How to **DRAW** people

This Book Belong To

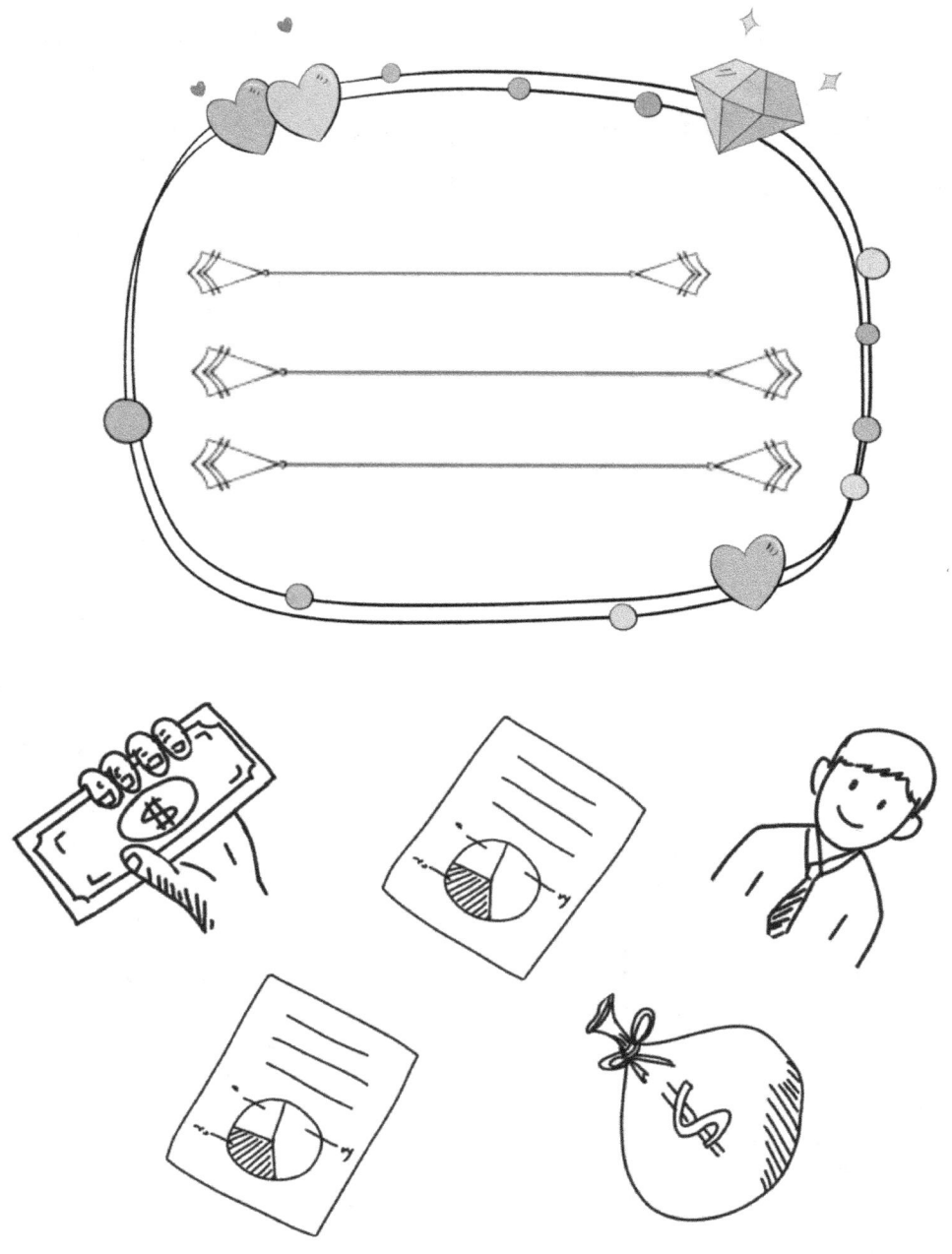

Circle the faces that show how you are feeling

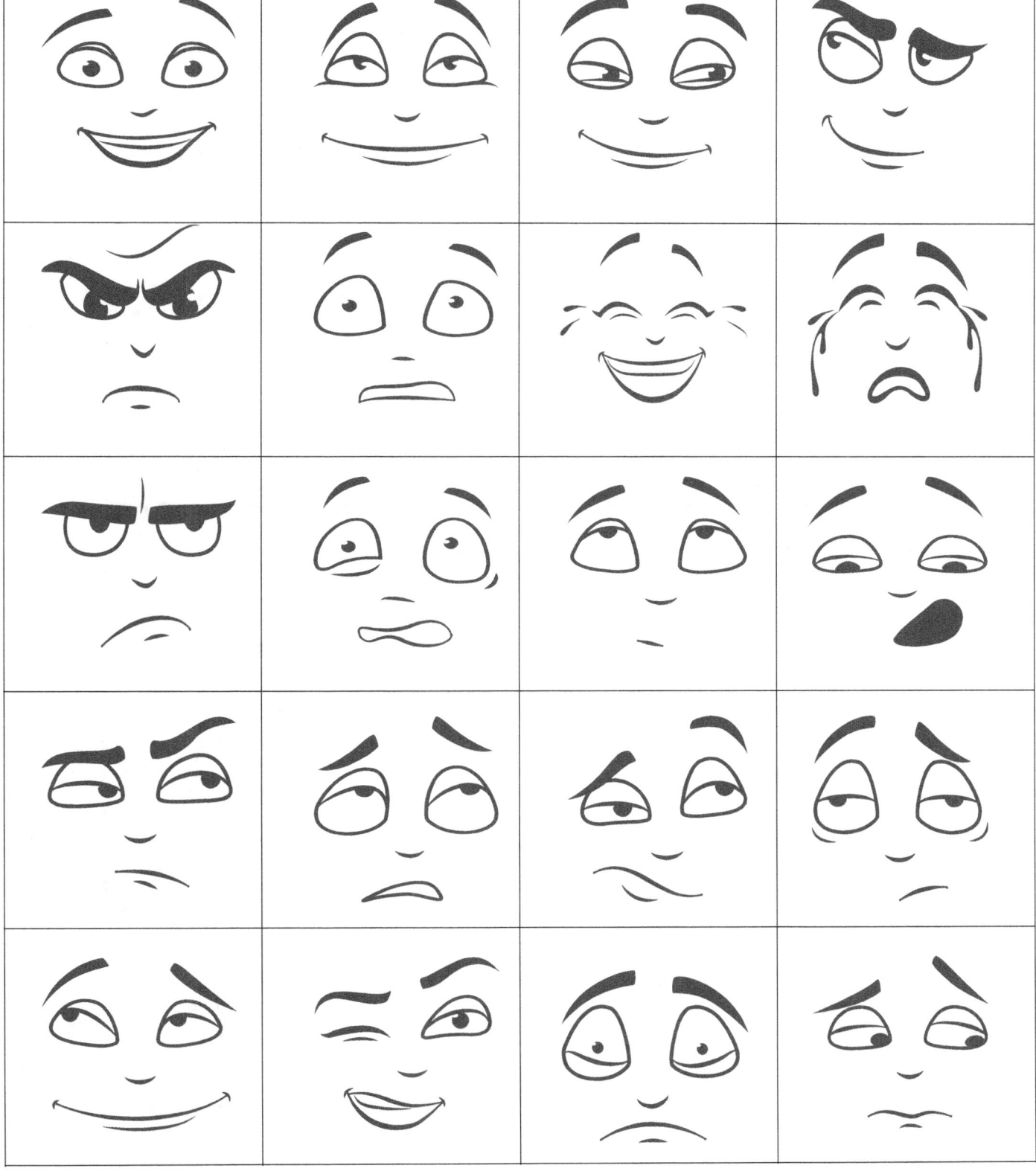

Content

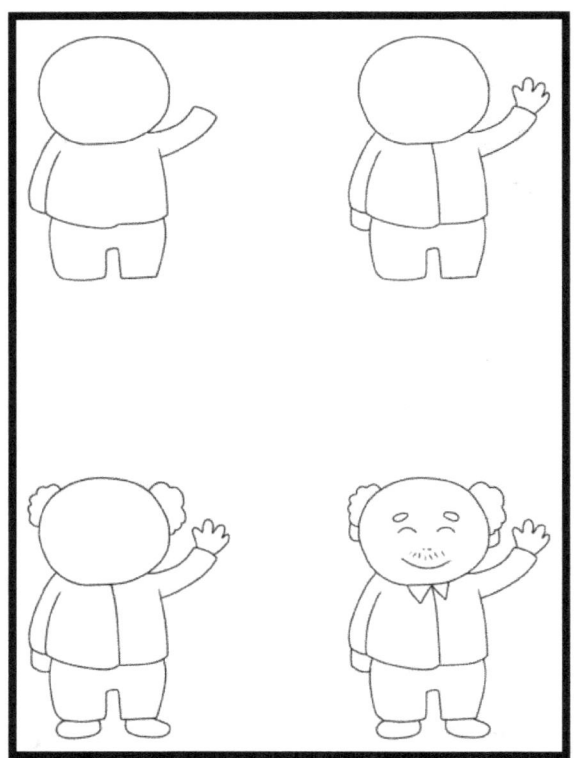 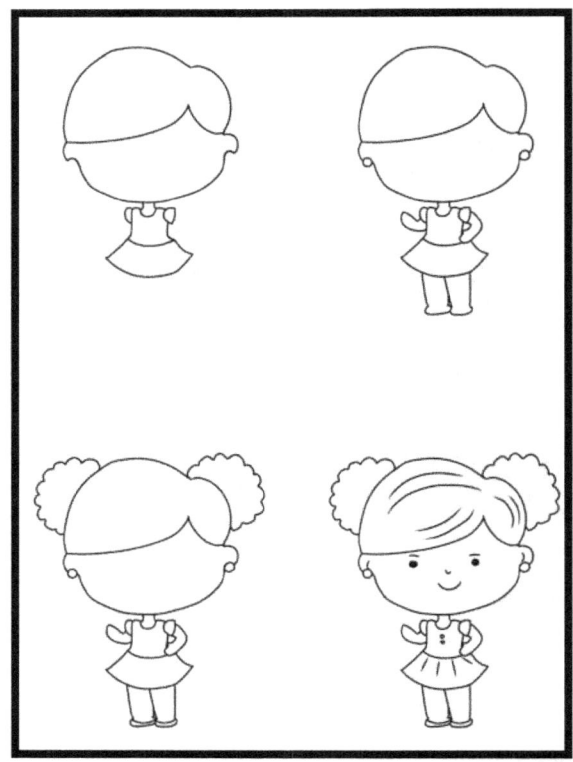

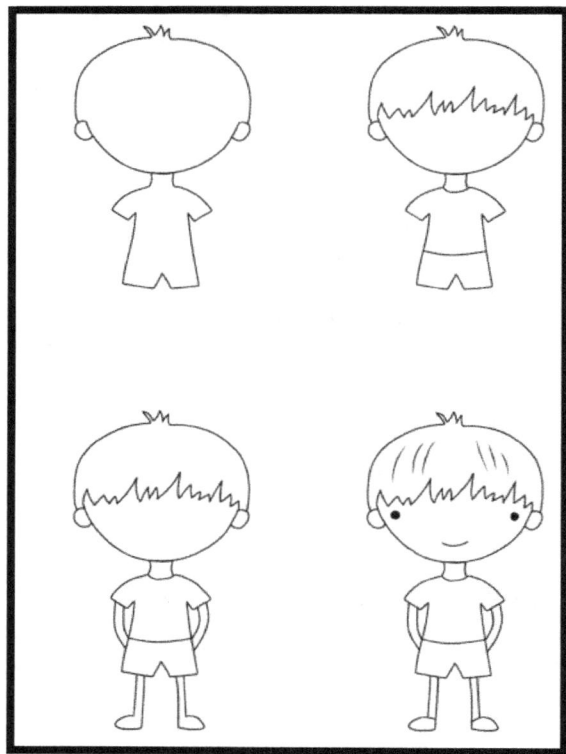 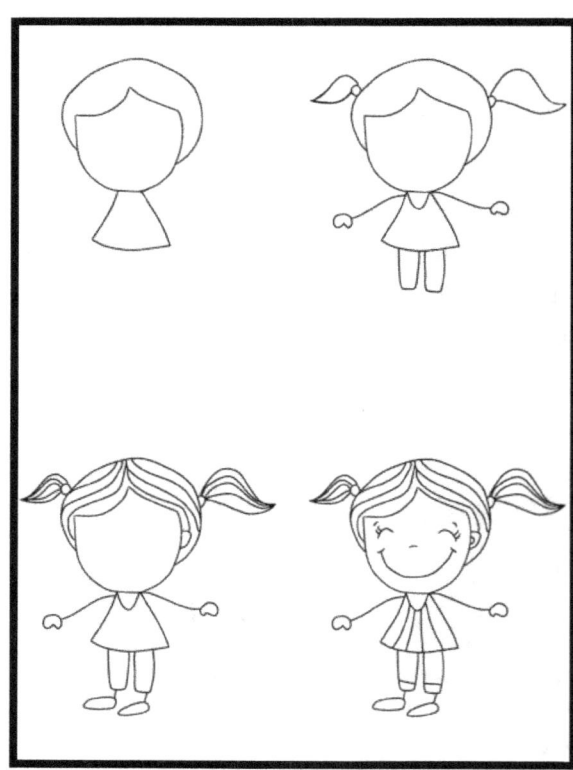

How to draw people

**thank you for your purchase,
we would be very grateful if you could leave
us a review**

for more book :

omiloveme Publishing

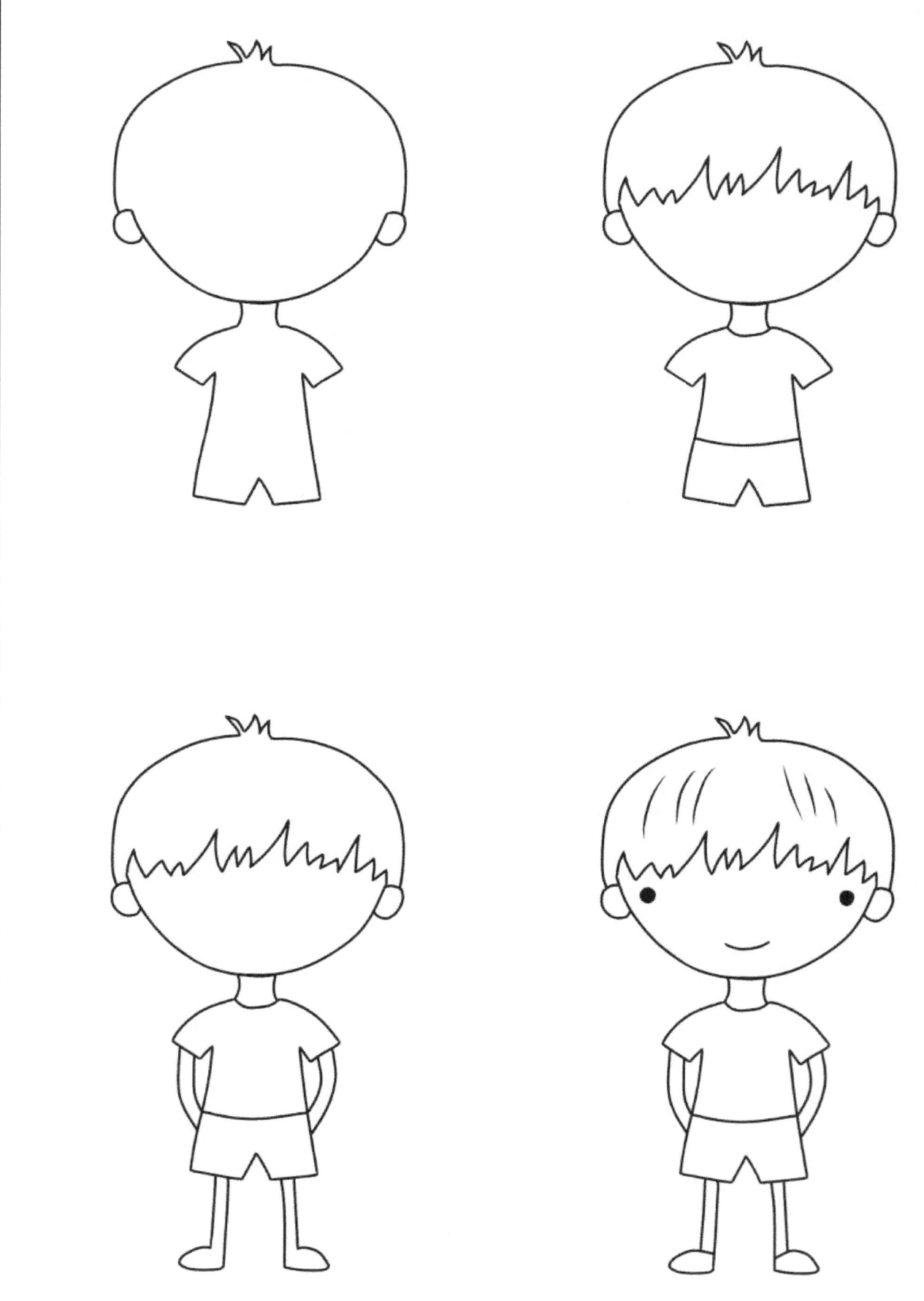

Now, it's your turn !

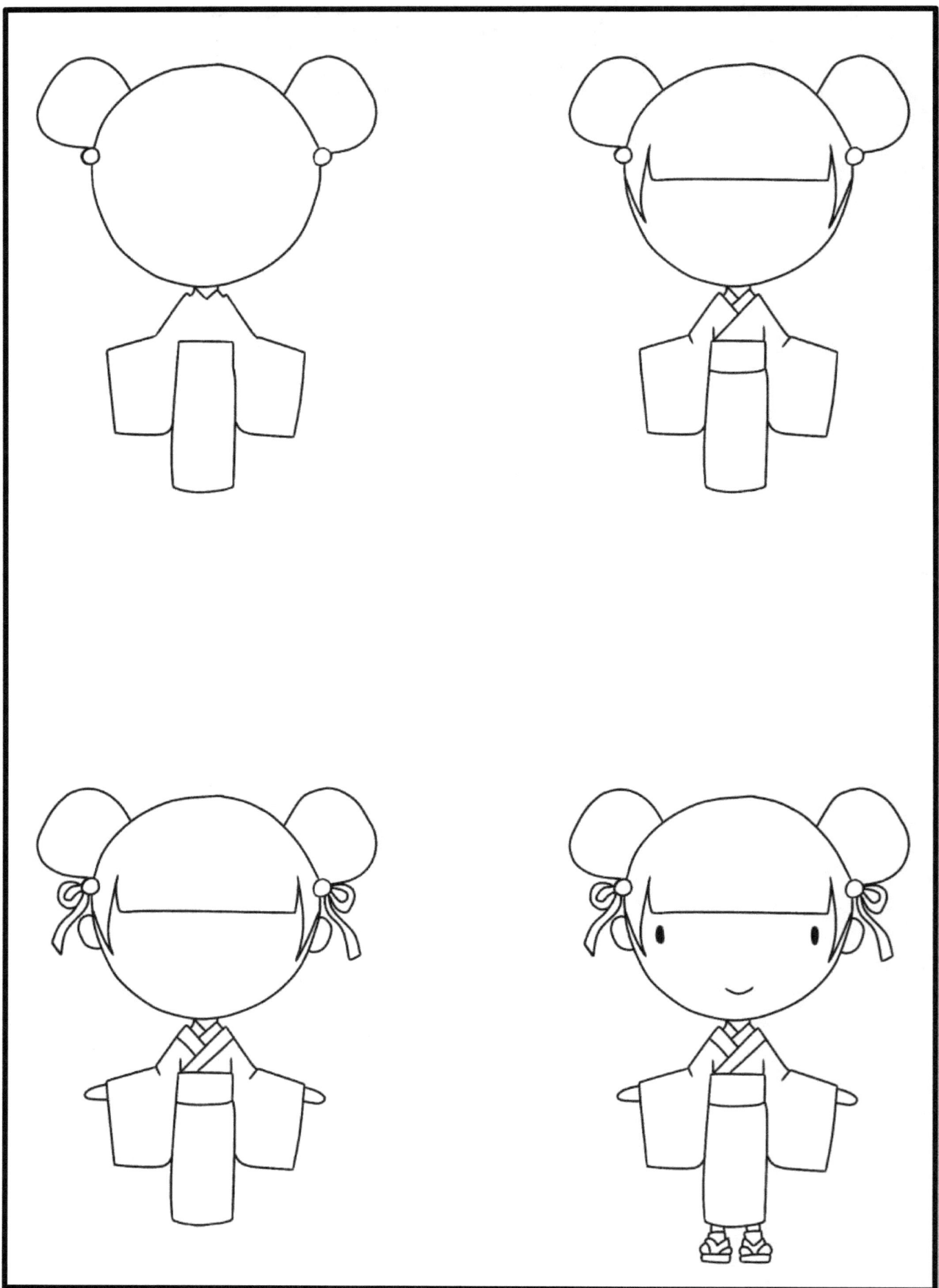

Now, it's your turn !

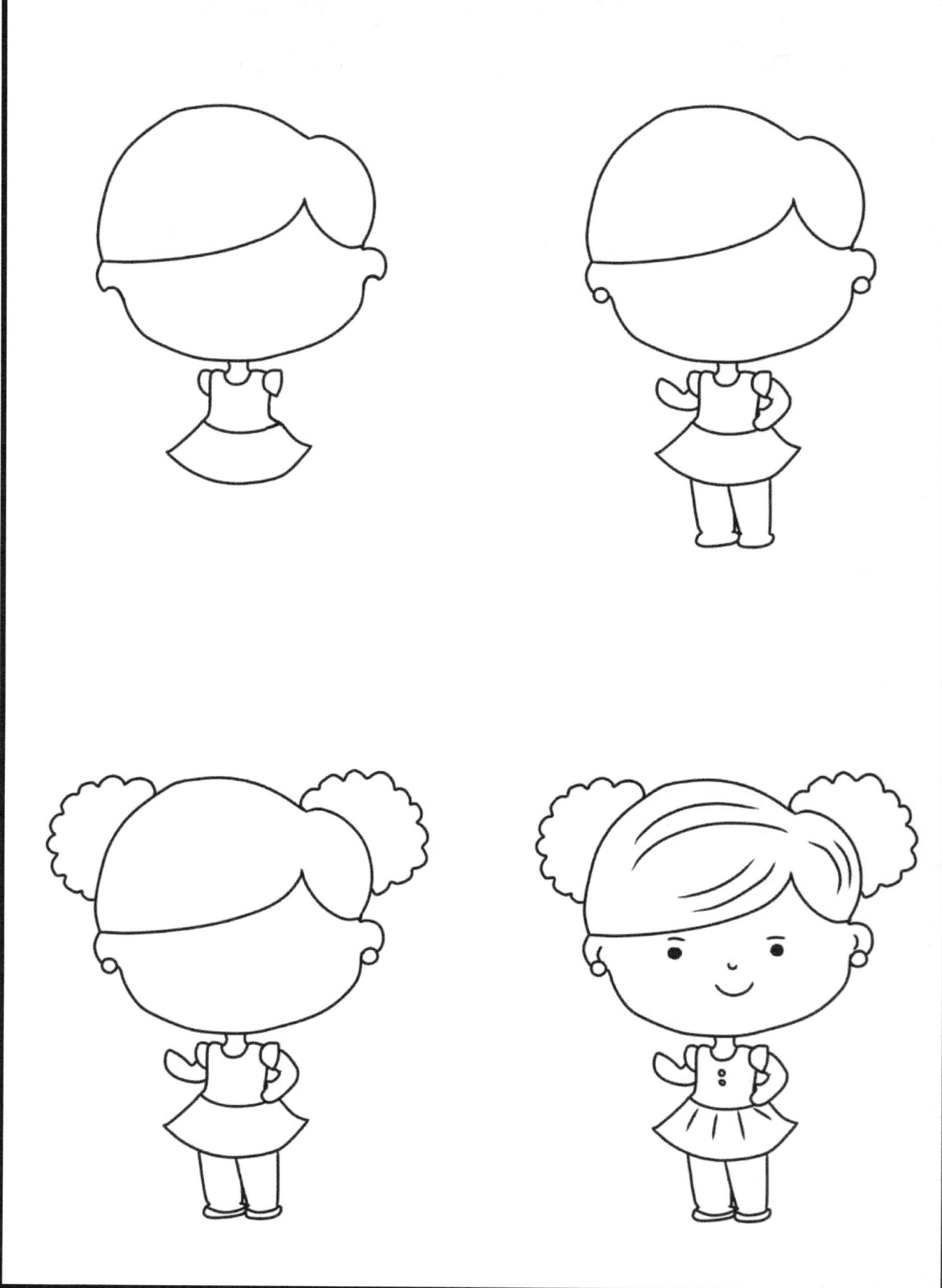

Now, it's your turn !

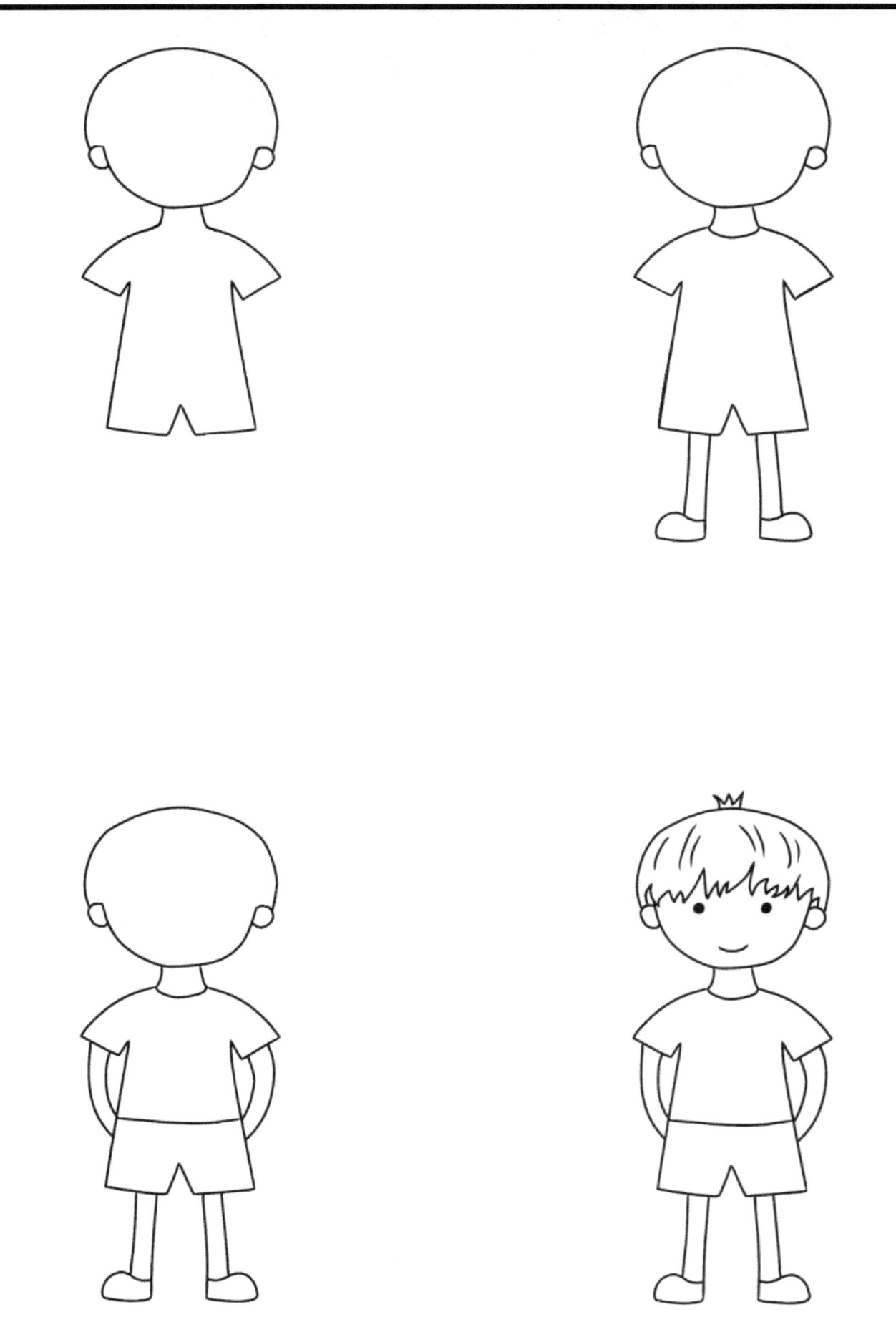

Now, it's your turn !

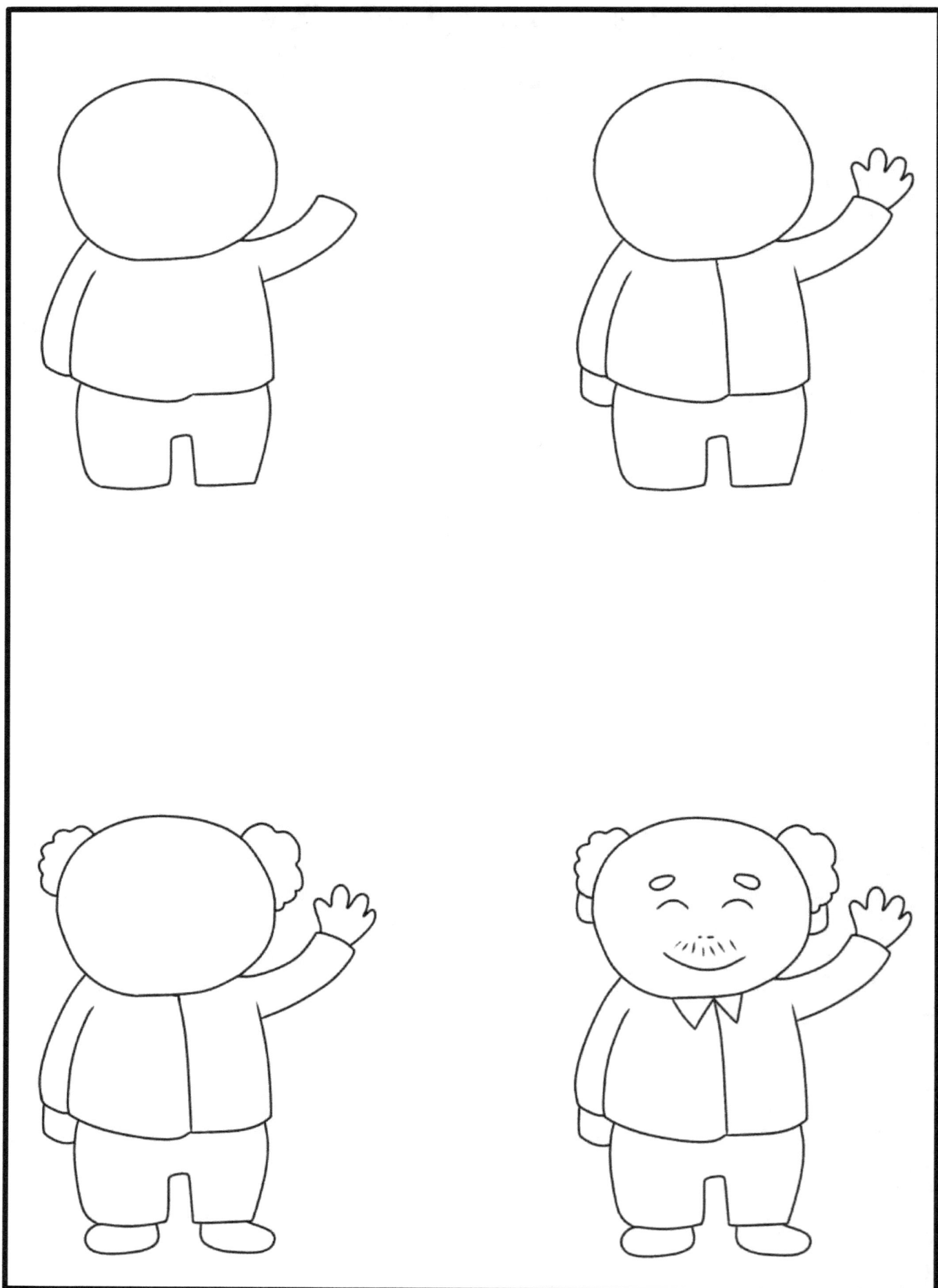

Now, it's your turn !

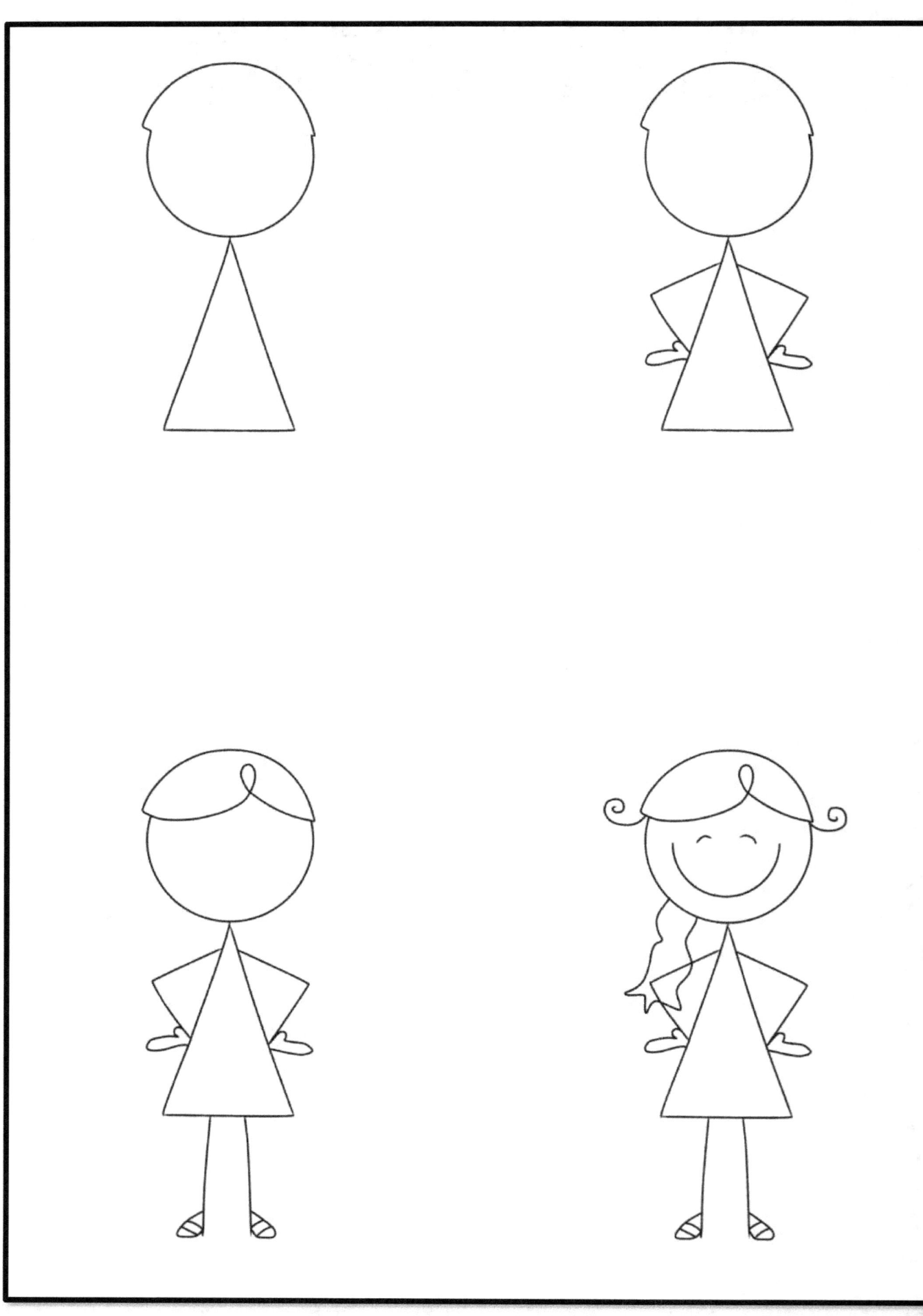

Now, it's your turn !

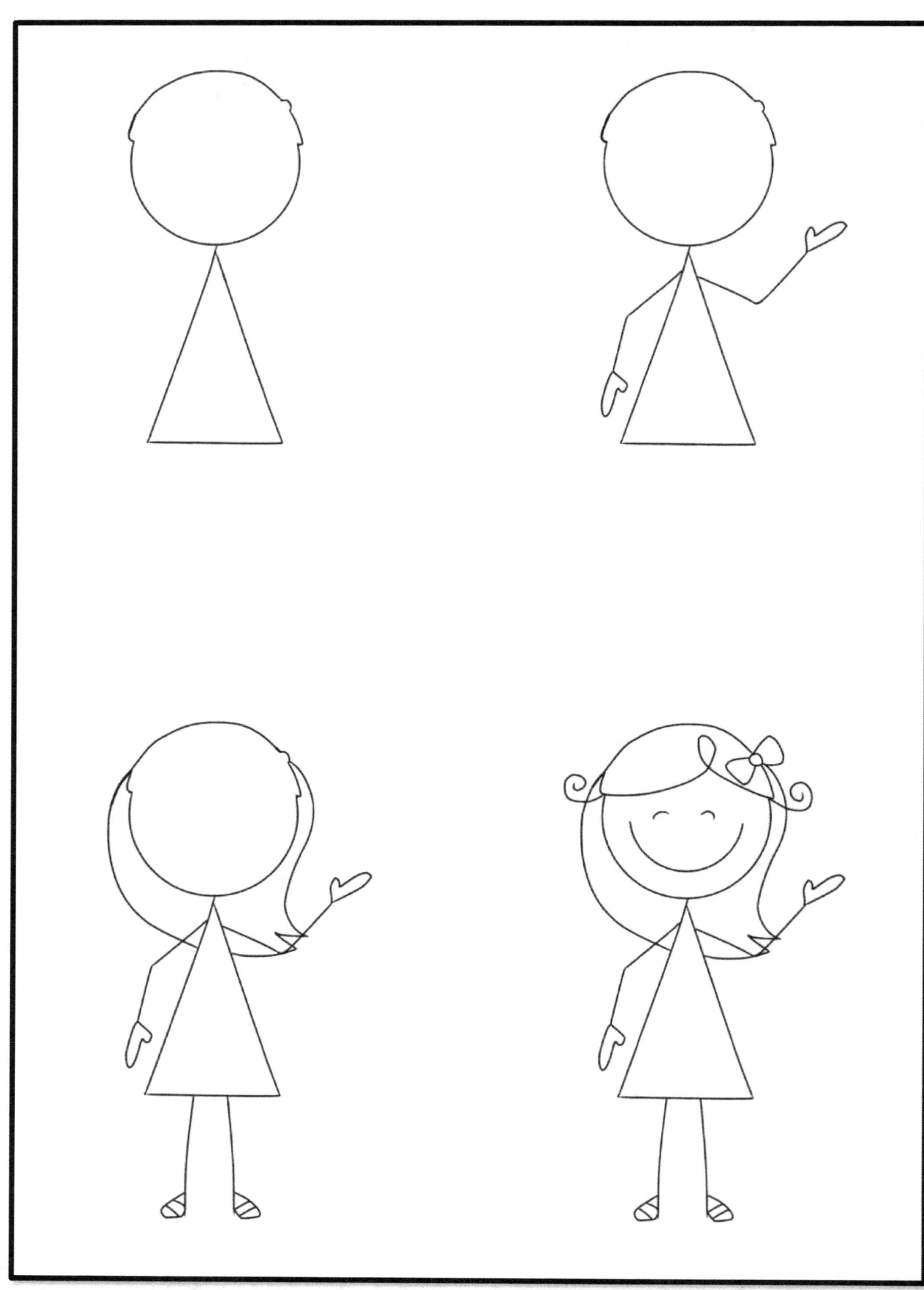

Now, it's your turn !

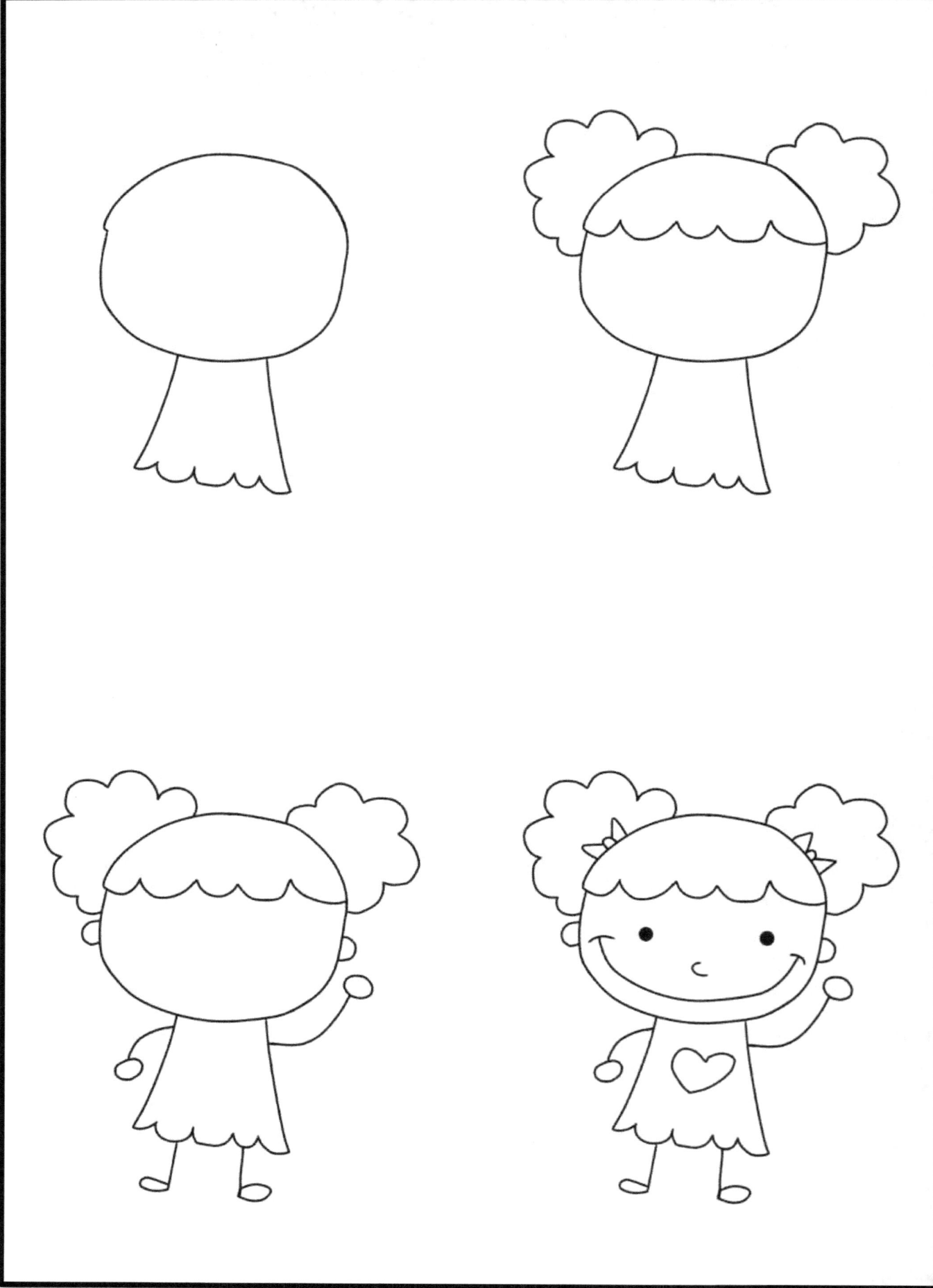

Now, it's your turn !

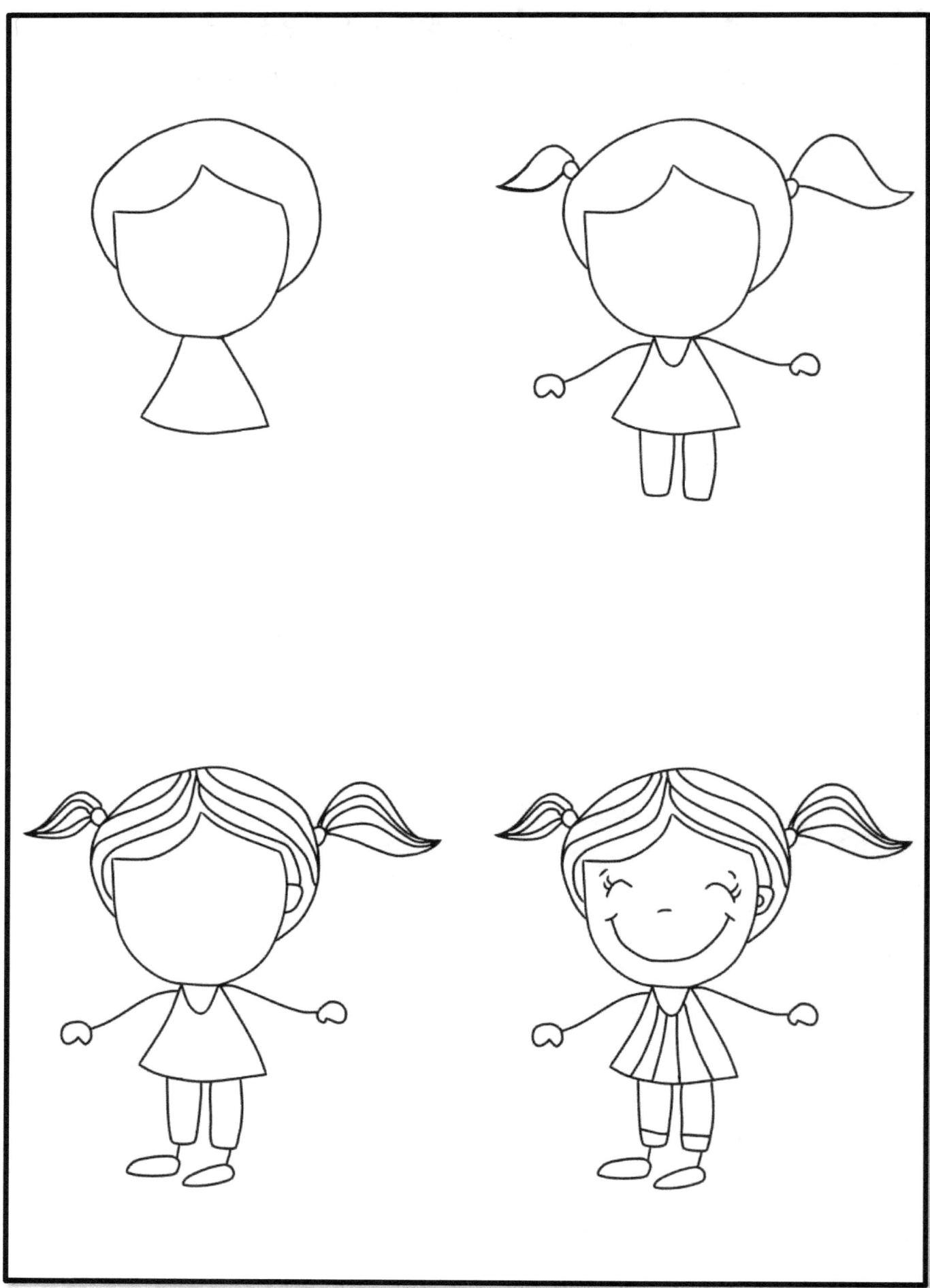

Now, it's your turn !

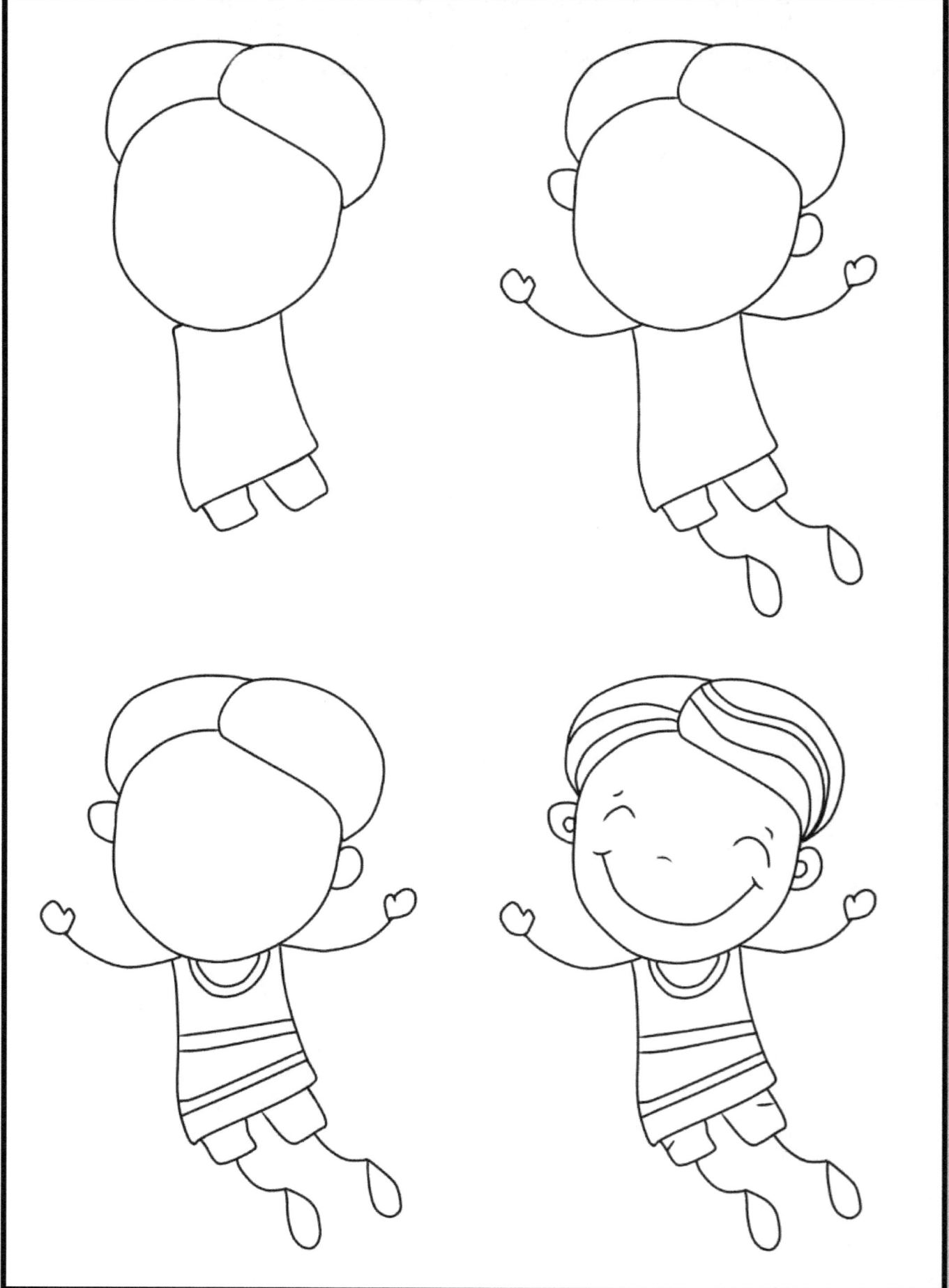

Now, it's your turn !

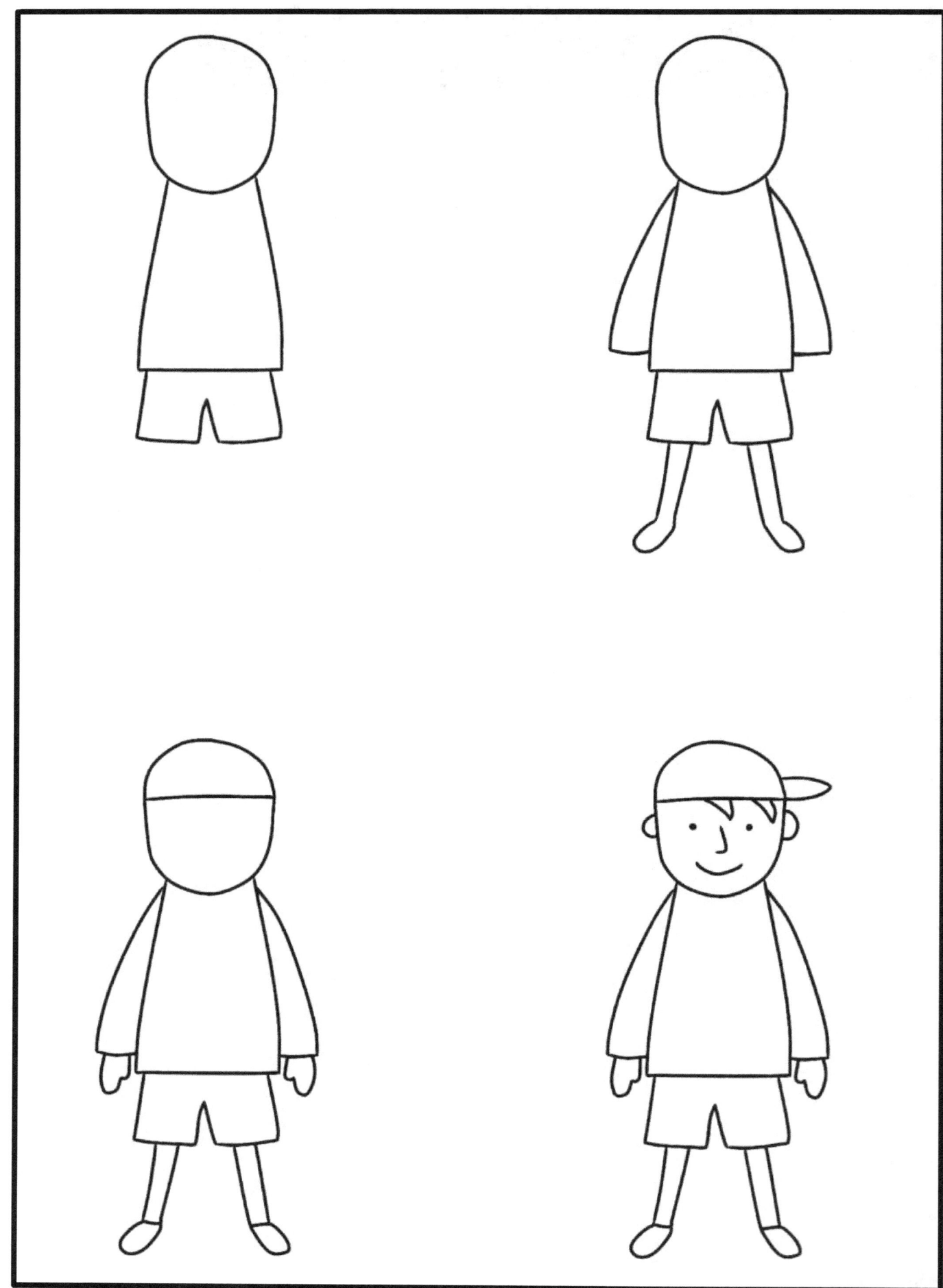

Now, it's your turn !

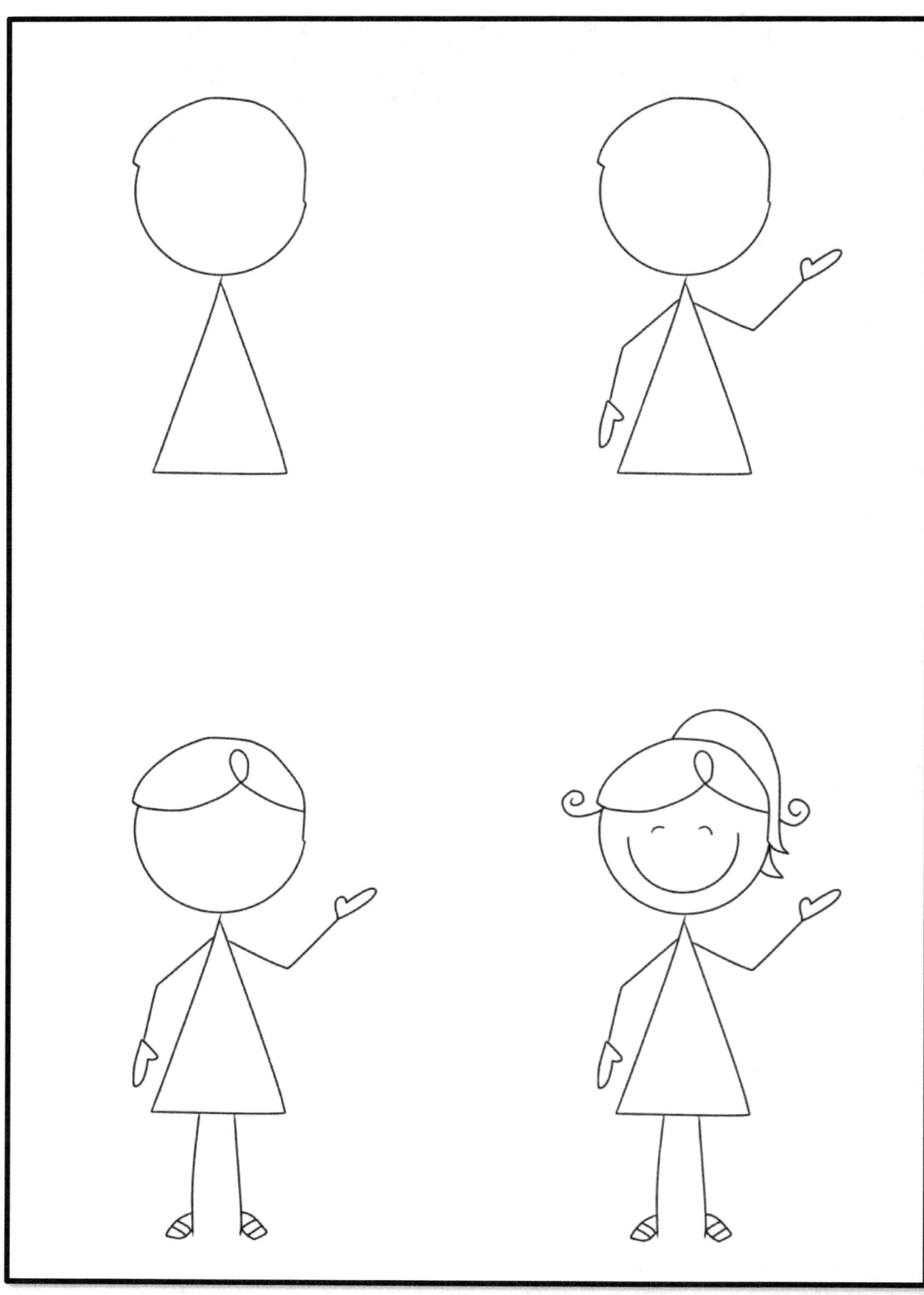

Now, it's your turn !

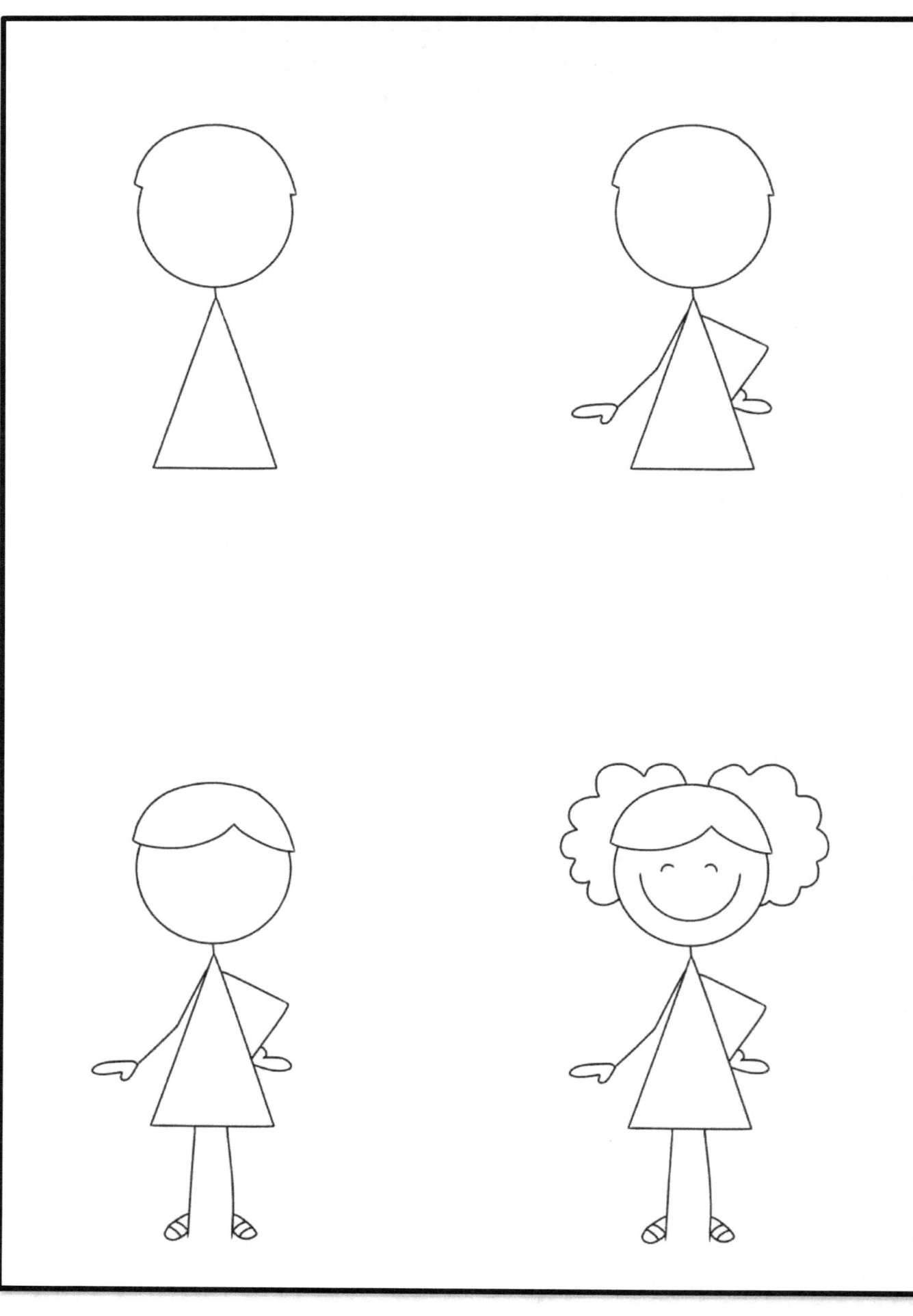

Now, it's your turn !

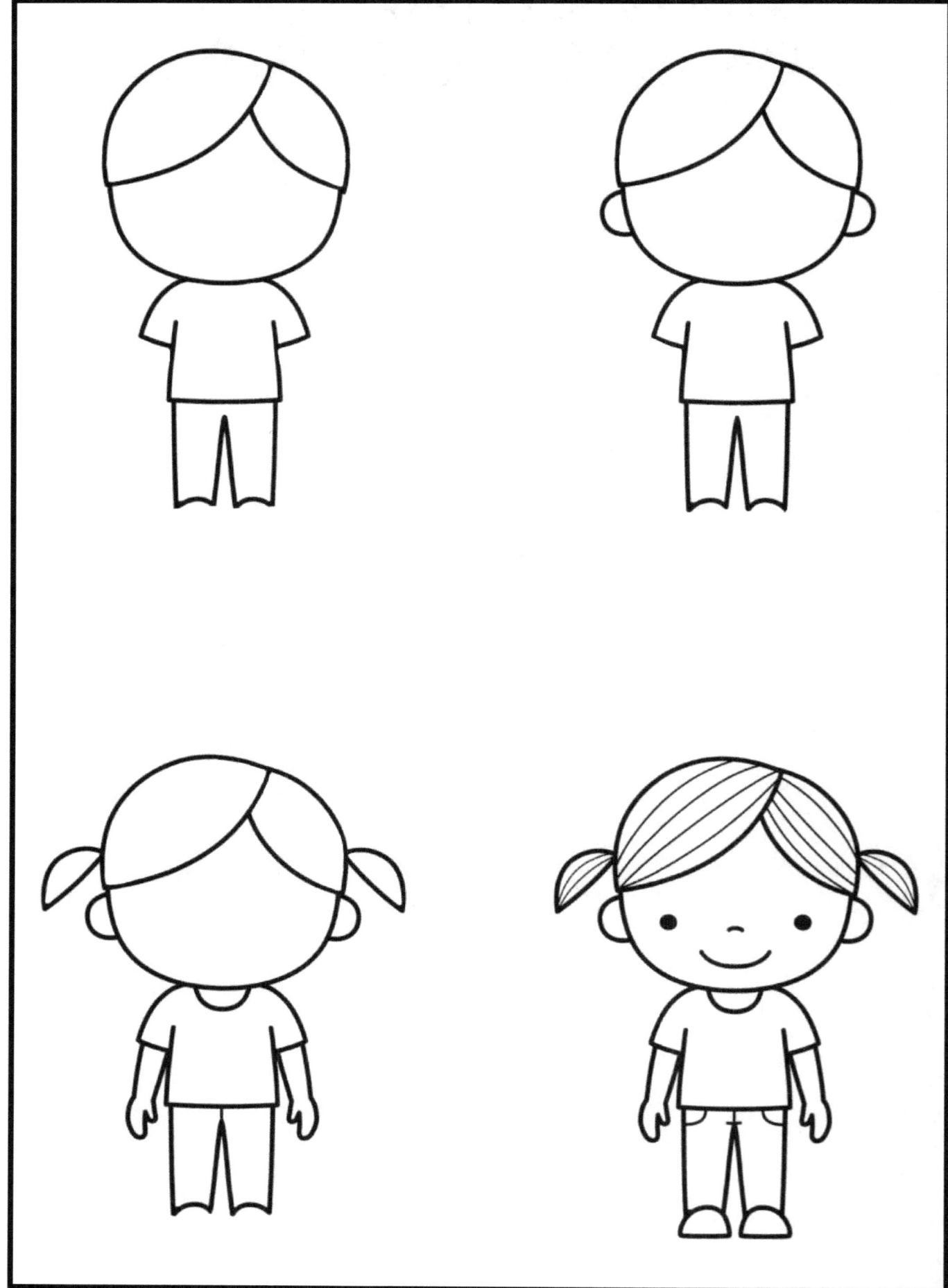

Now, it's your turn !

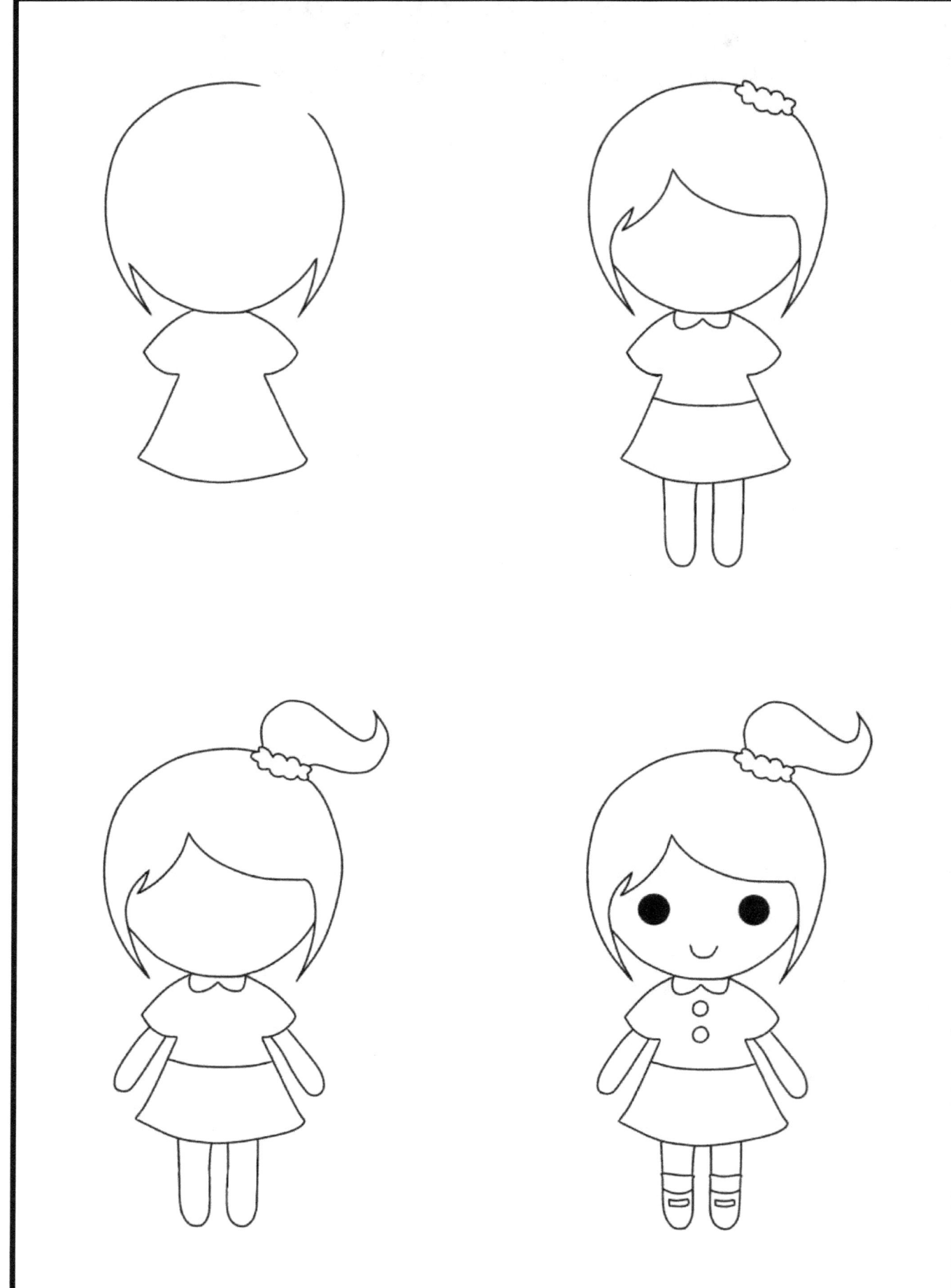

Now, it's your turn !

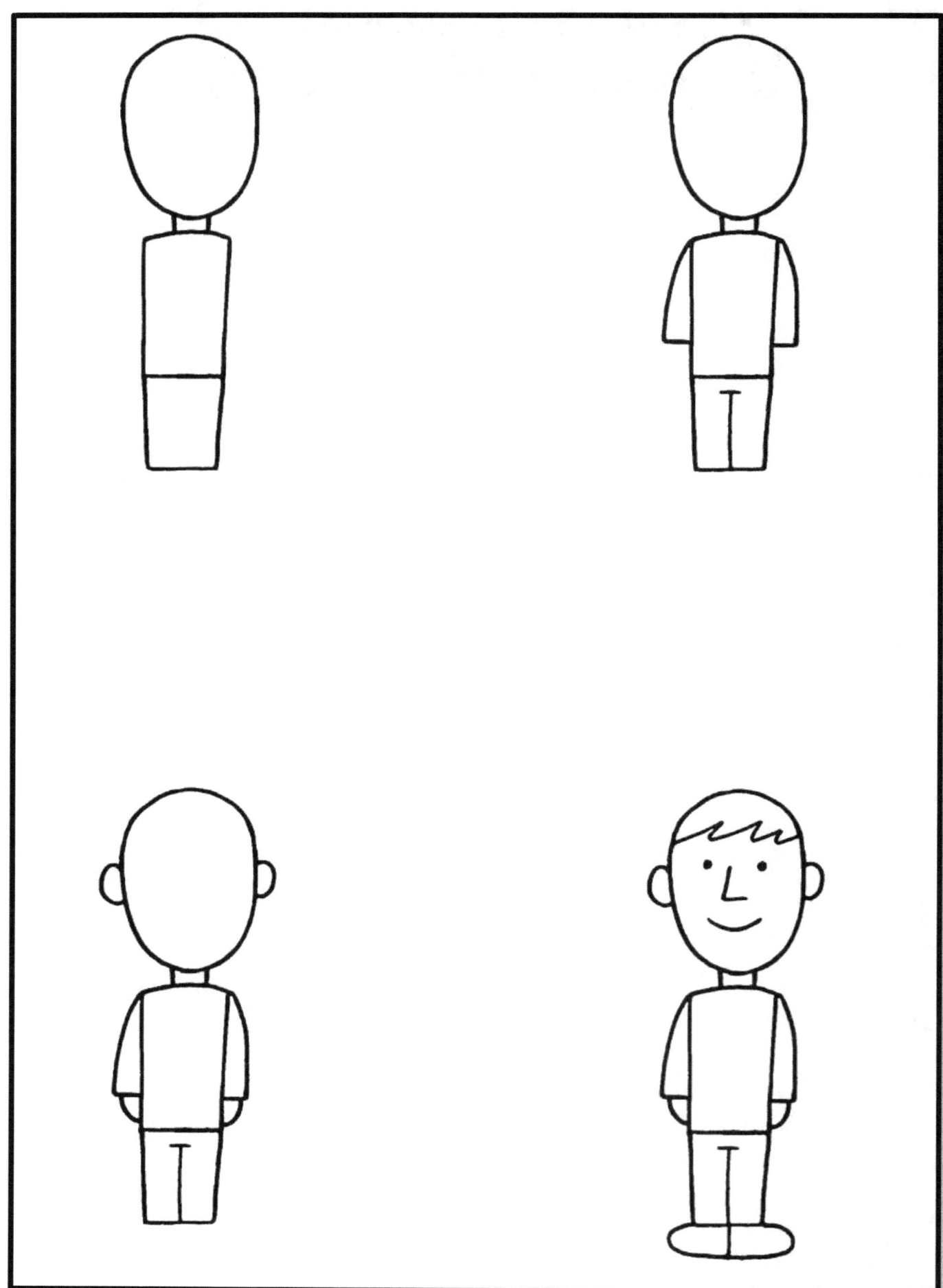

Now, it's your turn !

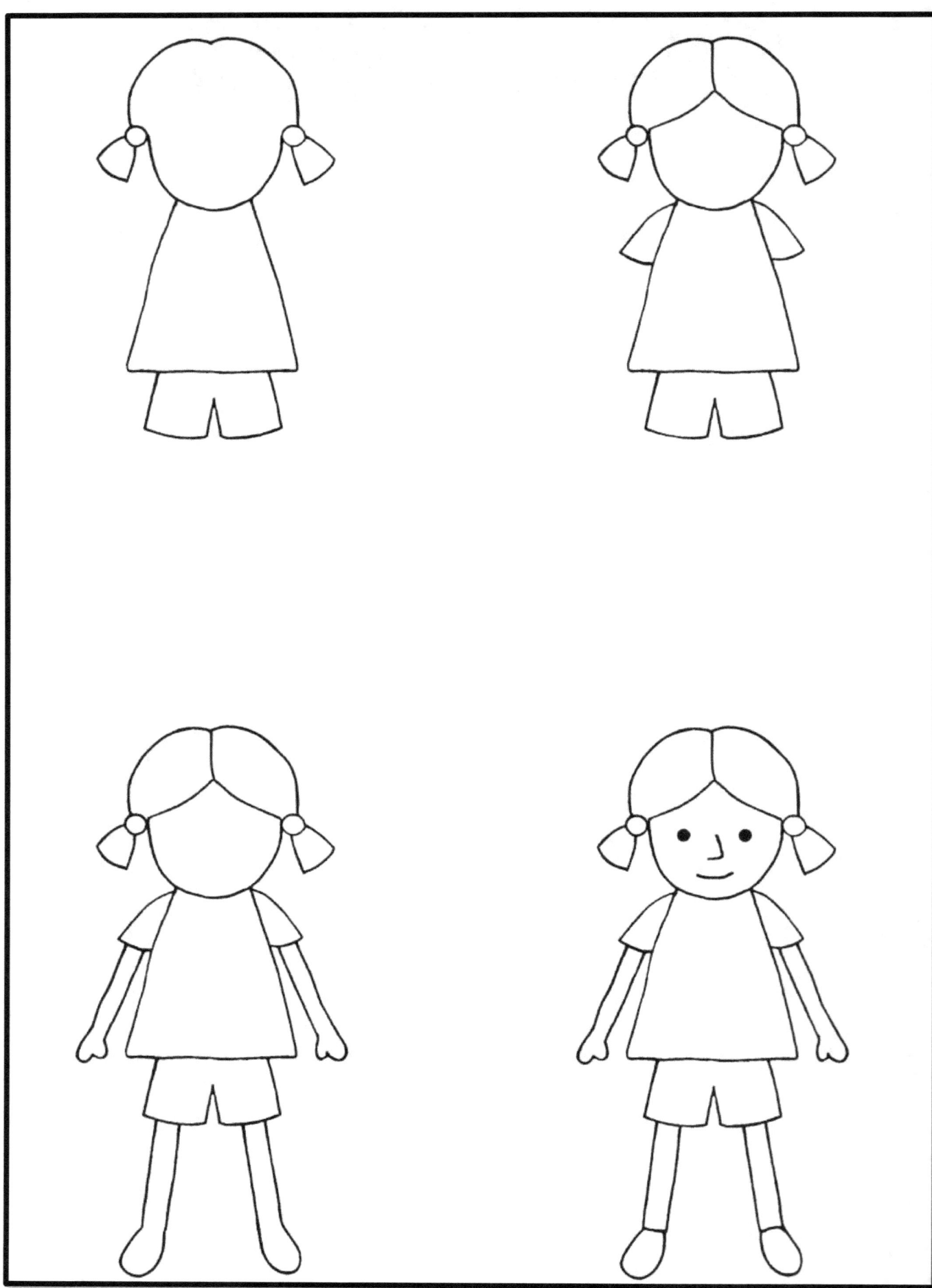

Now, it's your turn !

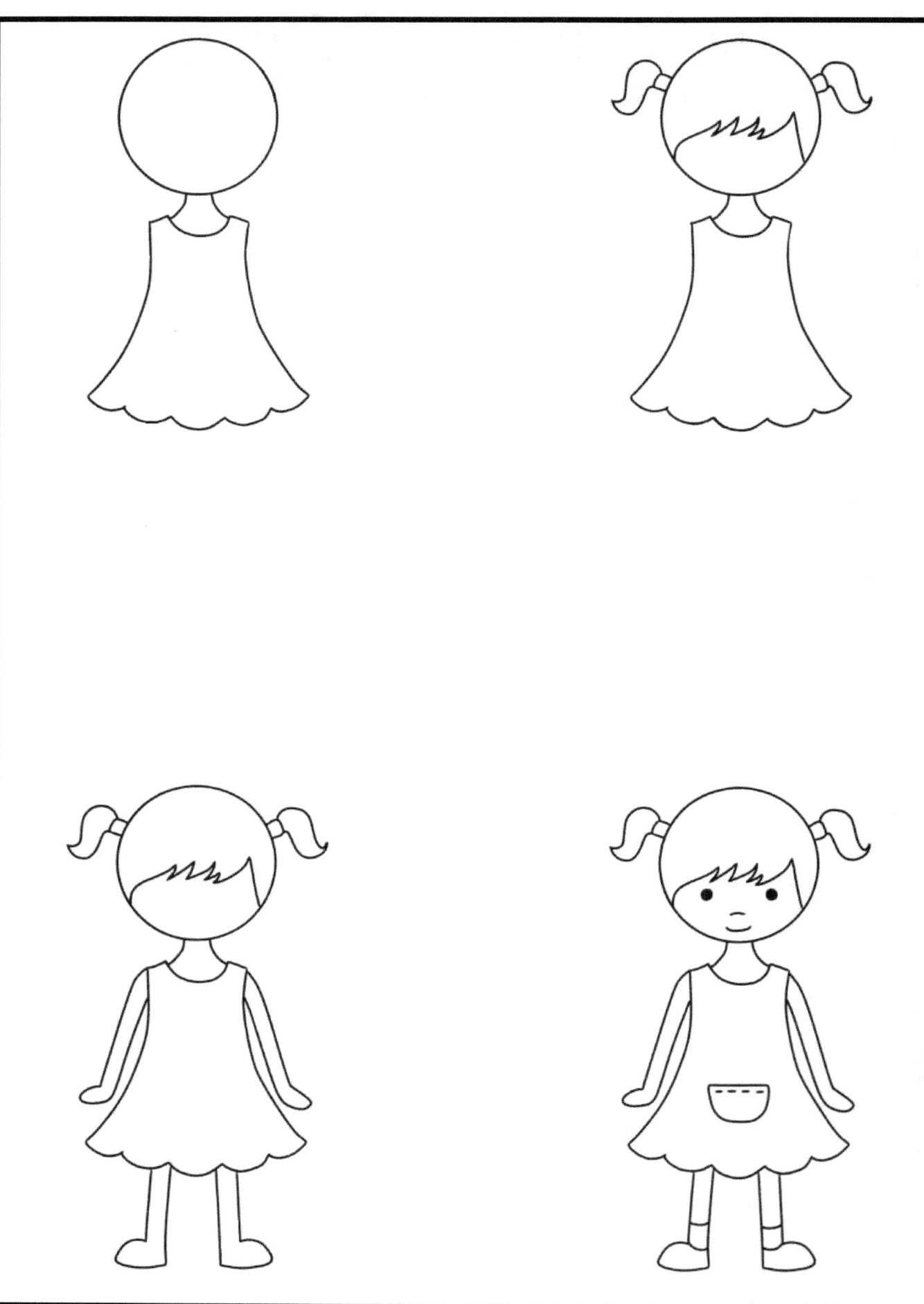

Now, it's your turn !

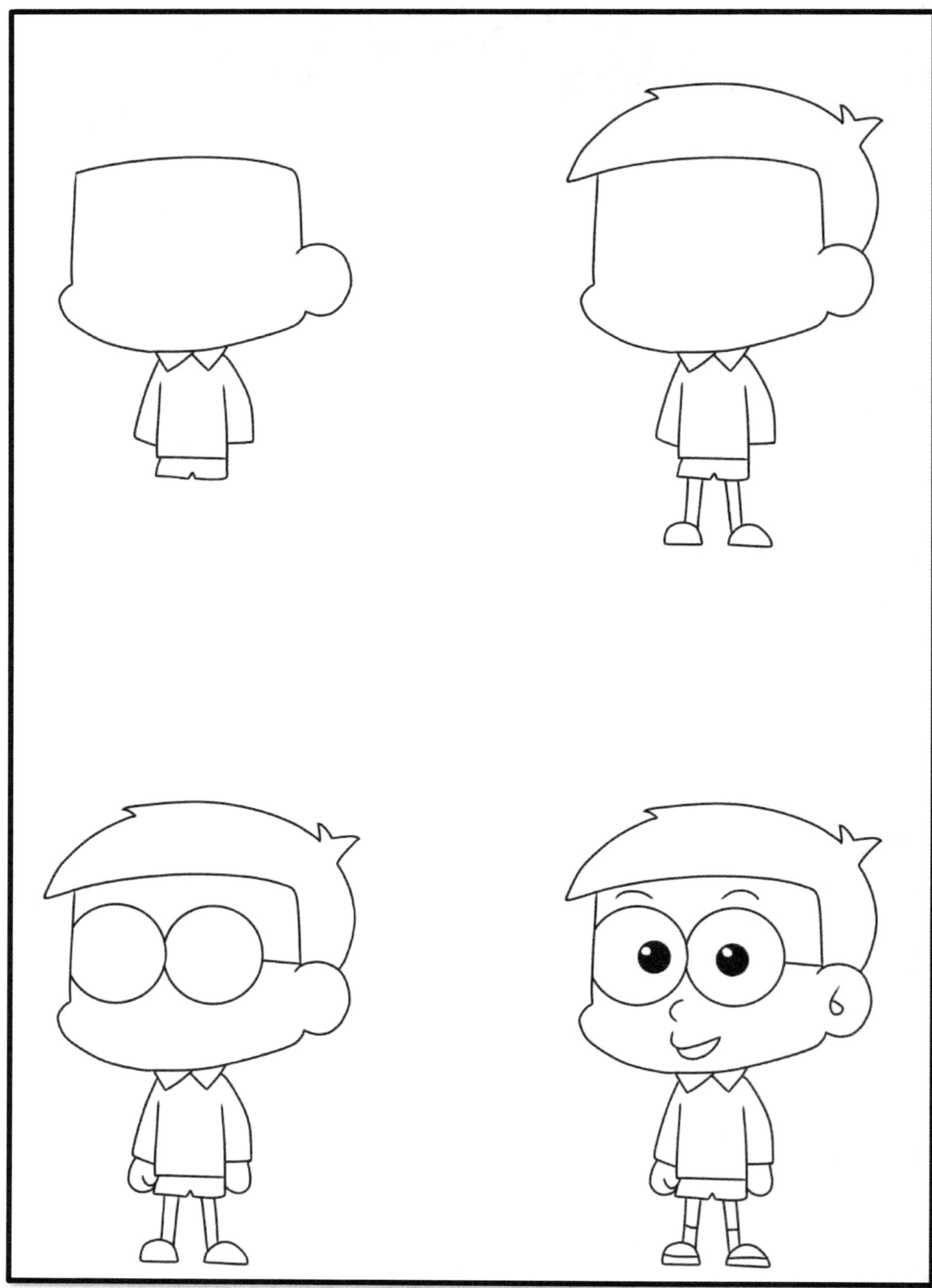

Now, it's your turn !

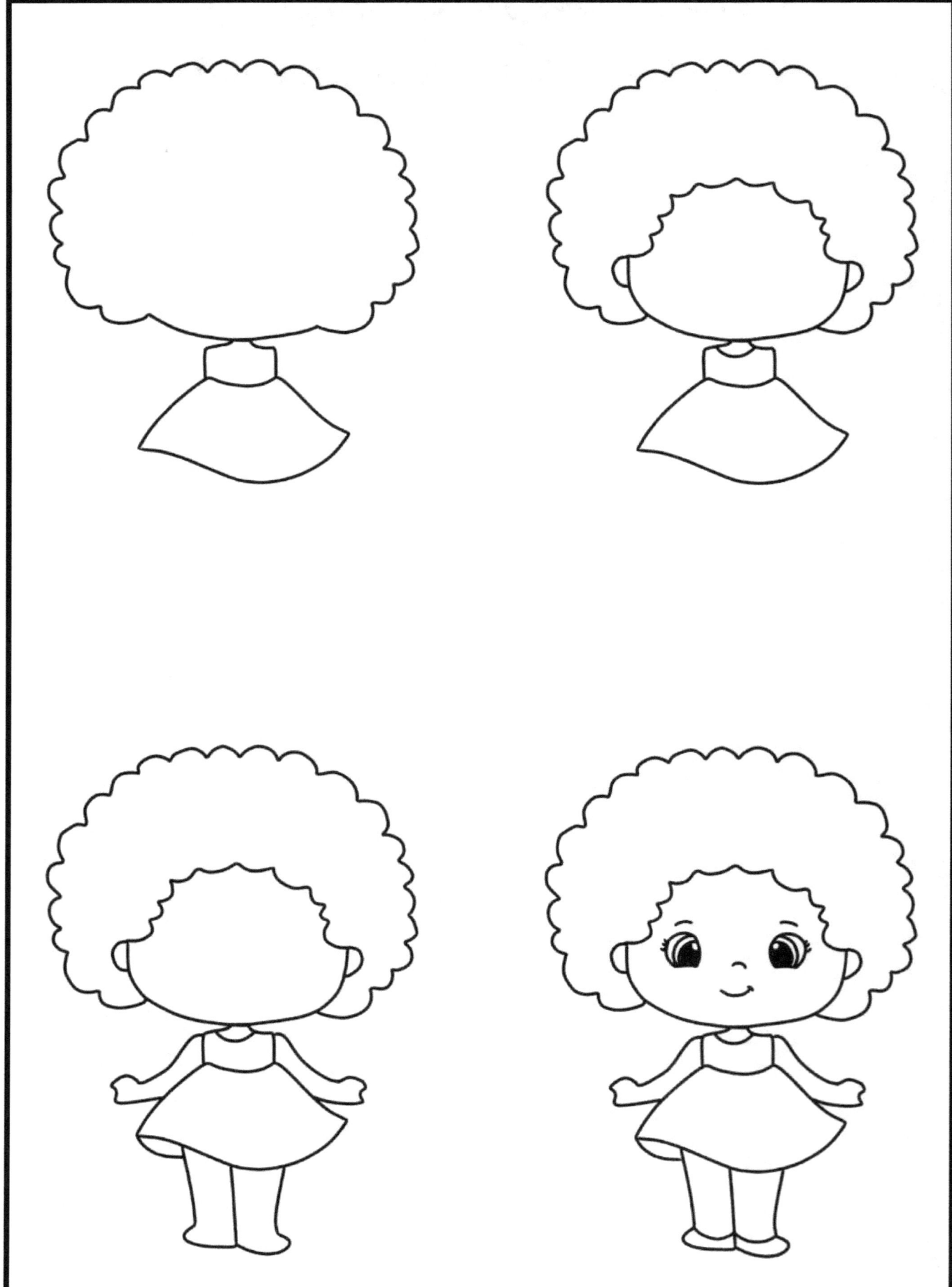

Now, it's your turn !

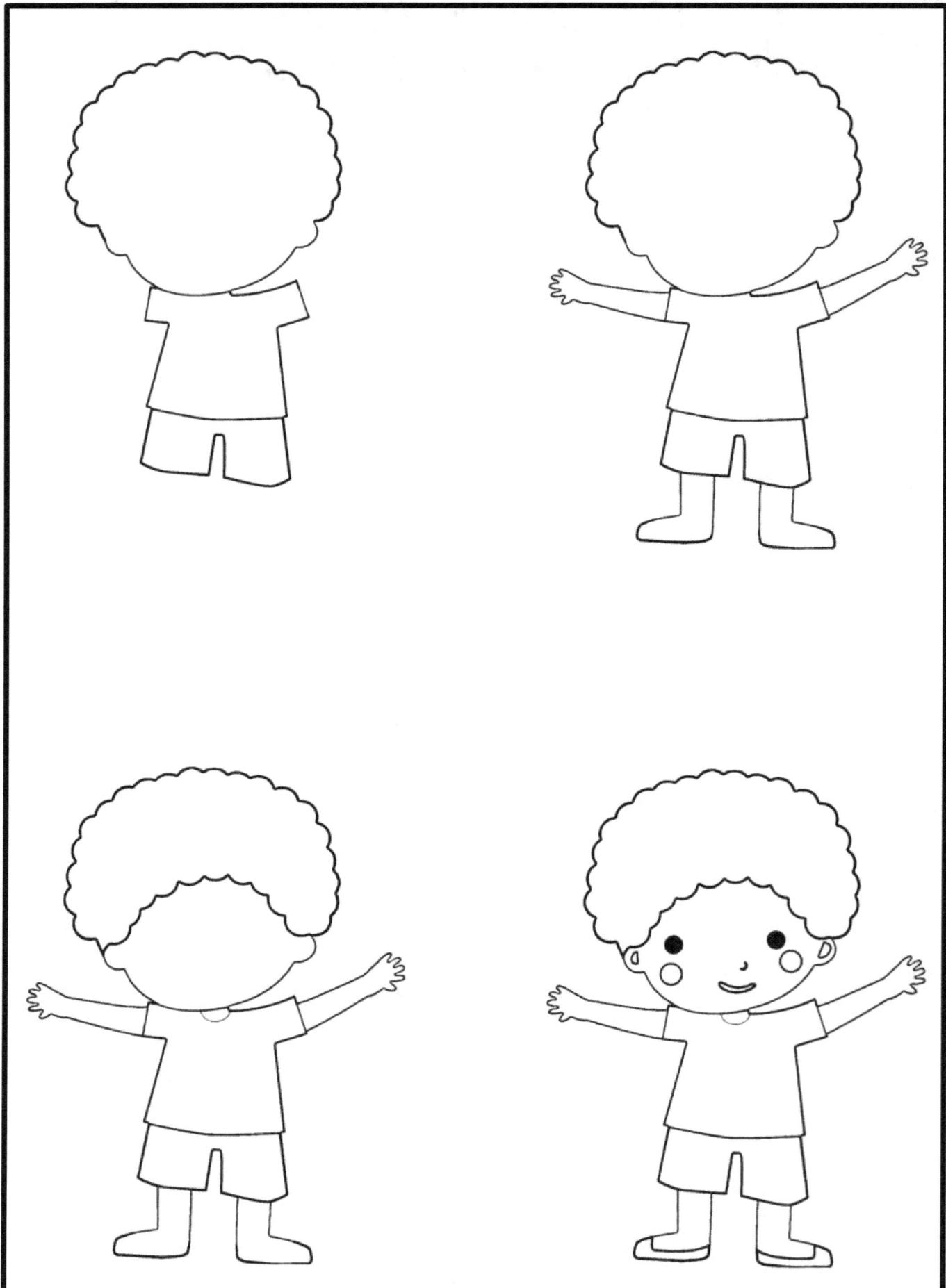

Now, it's your turn !

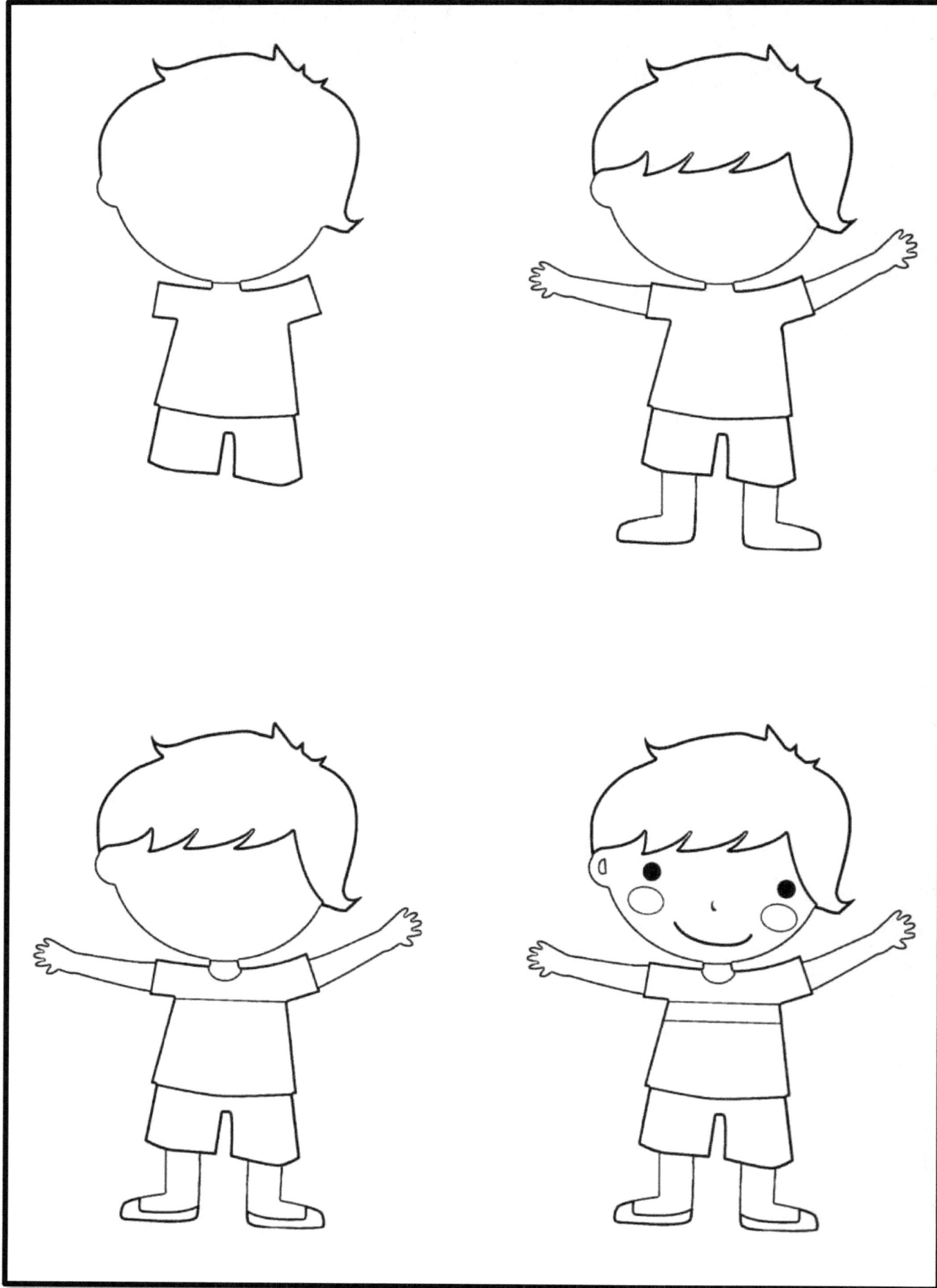

Now, it's your turn !

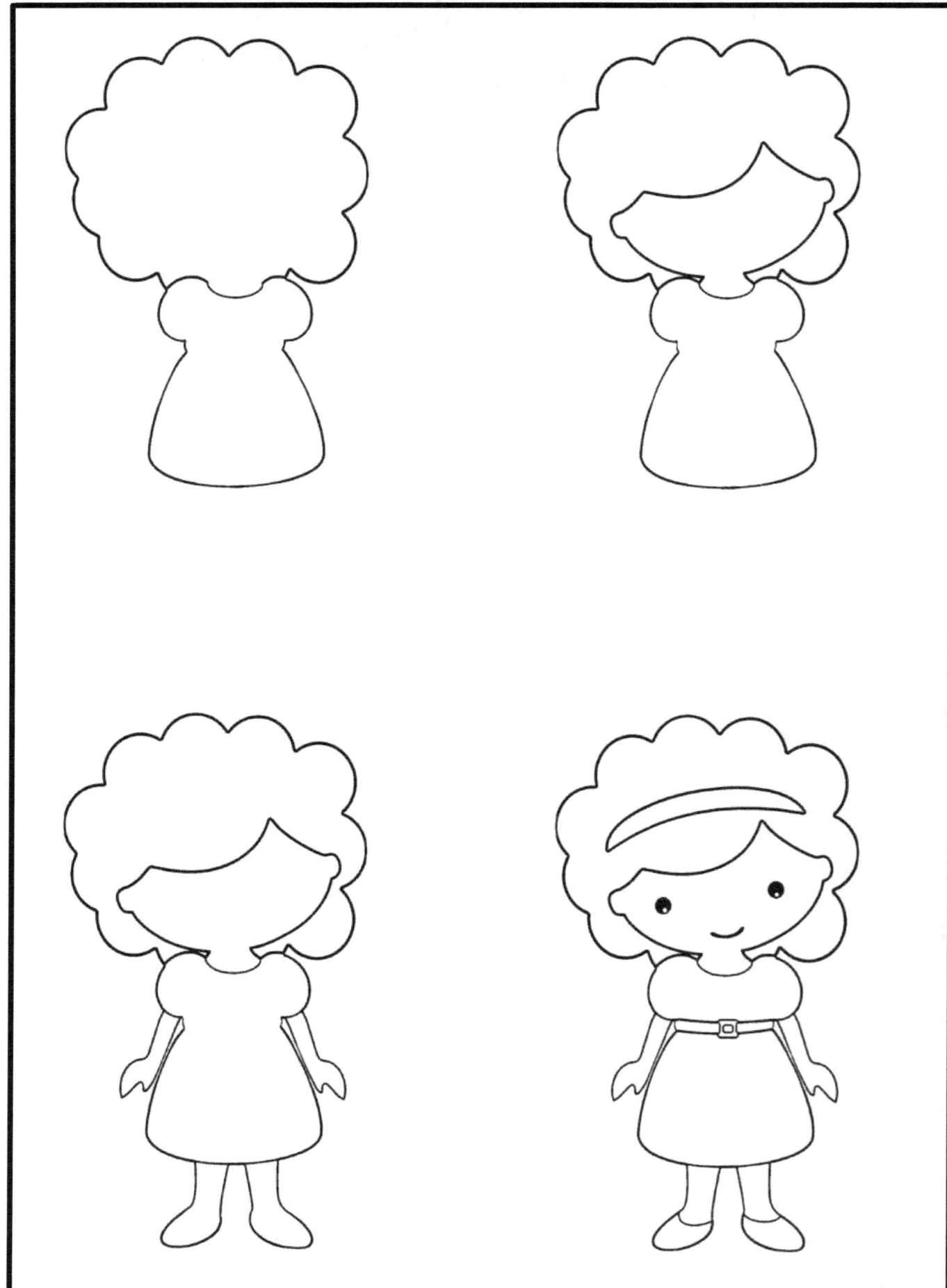

Now, it's your turn !

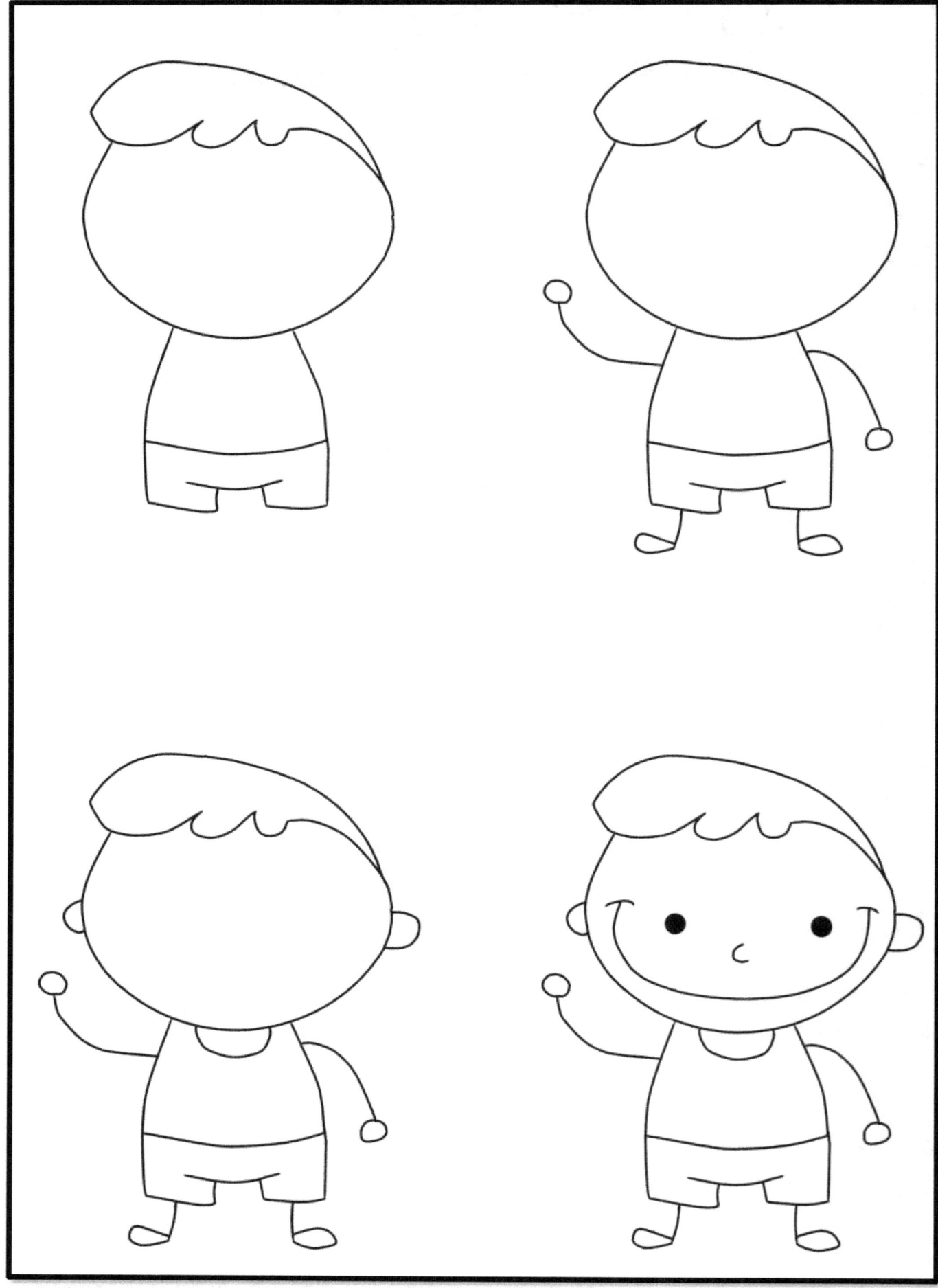

Now, it's your turn !

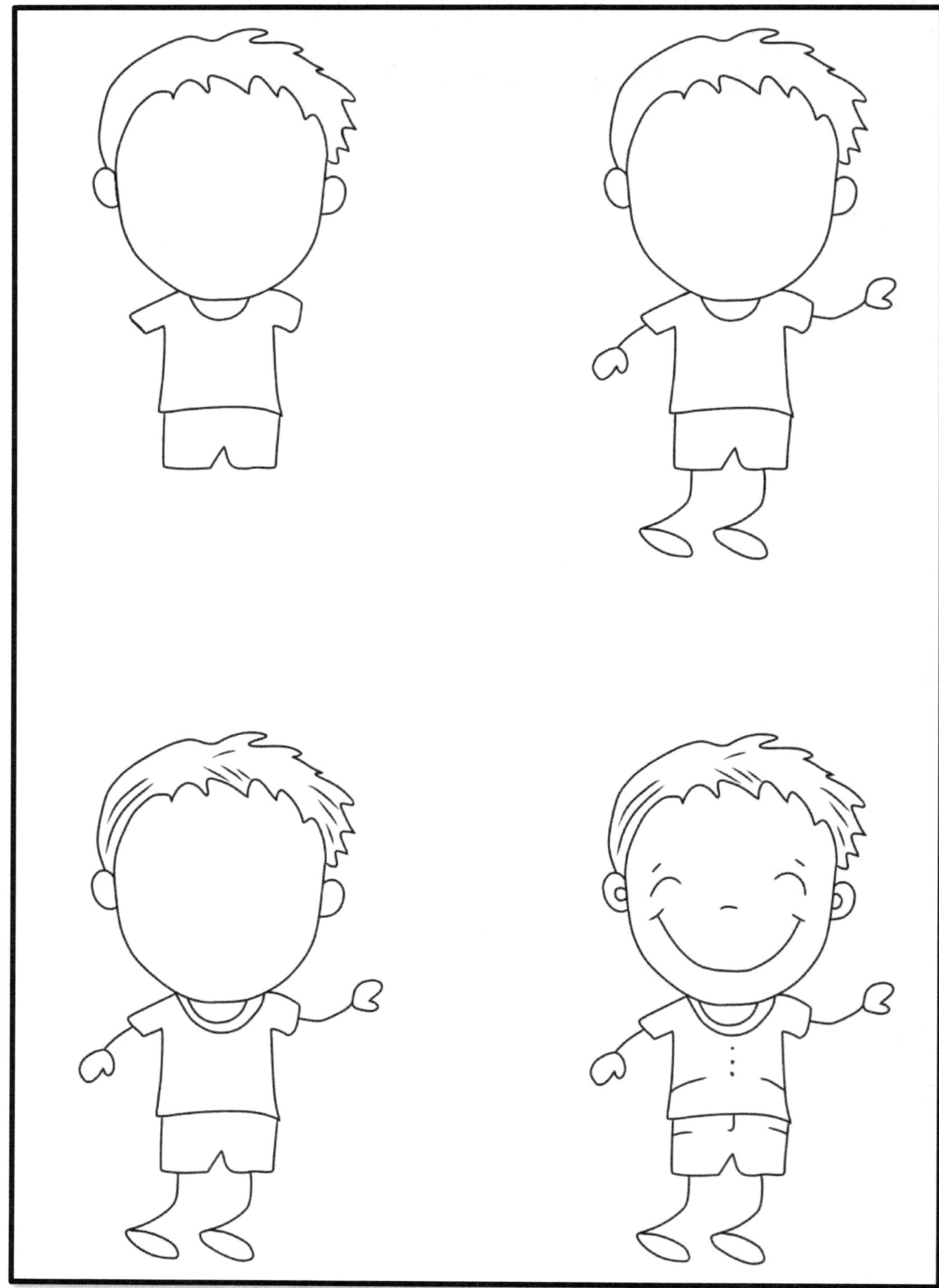

Now, it's your turn !

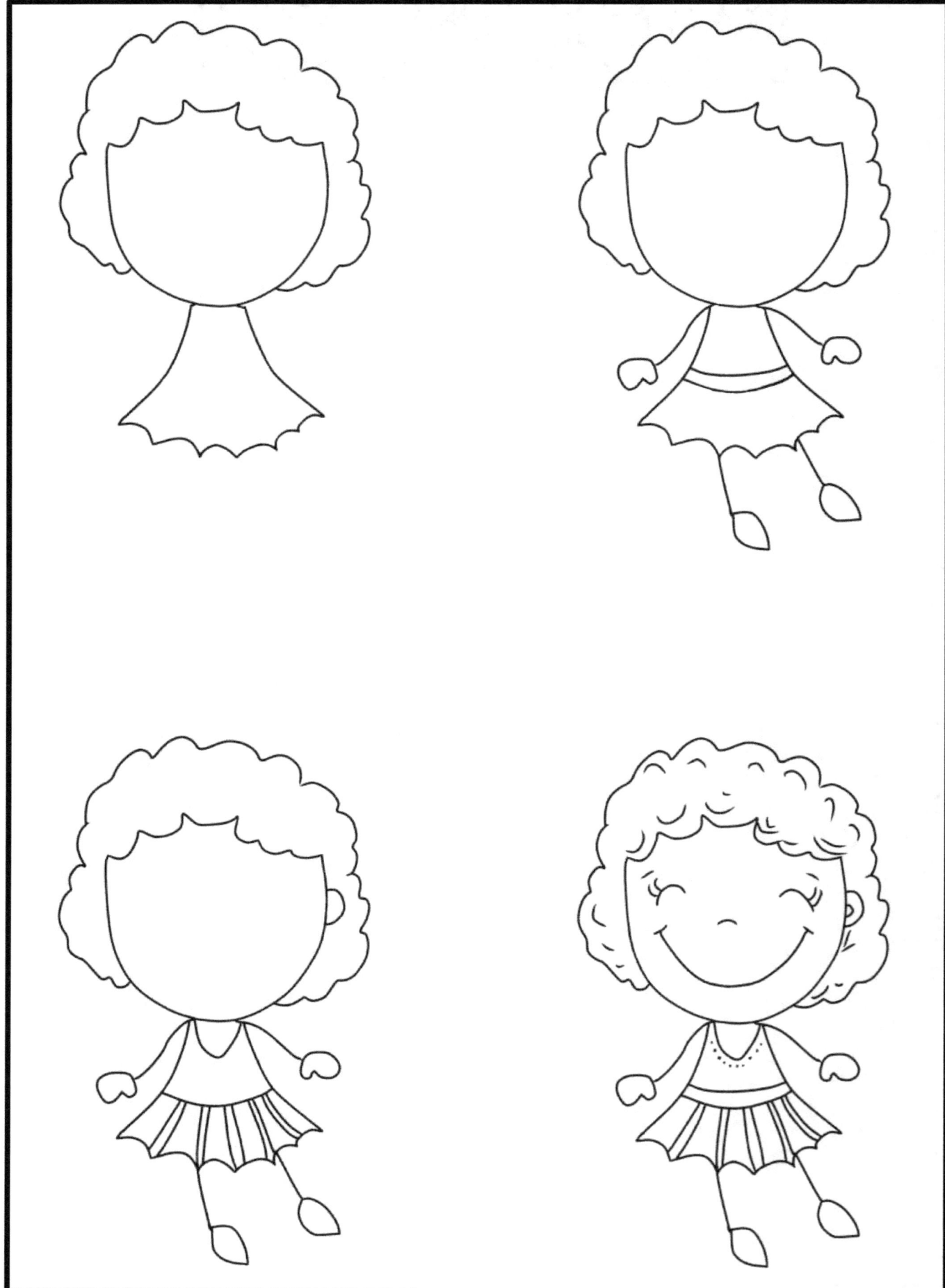

Now, it's your turn !

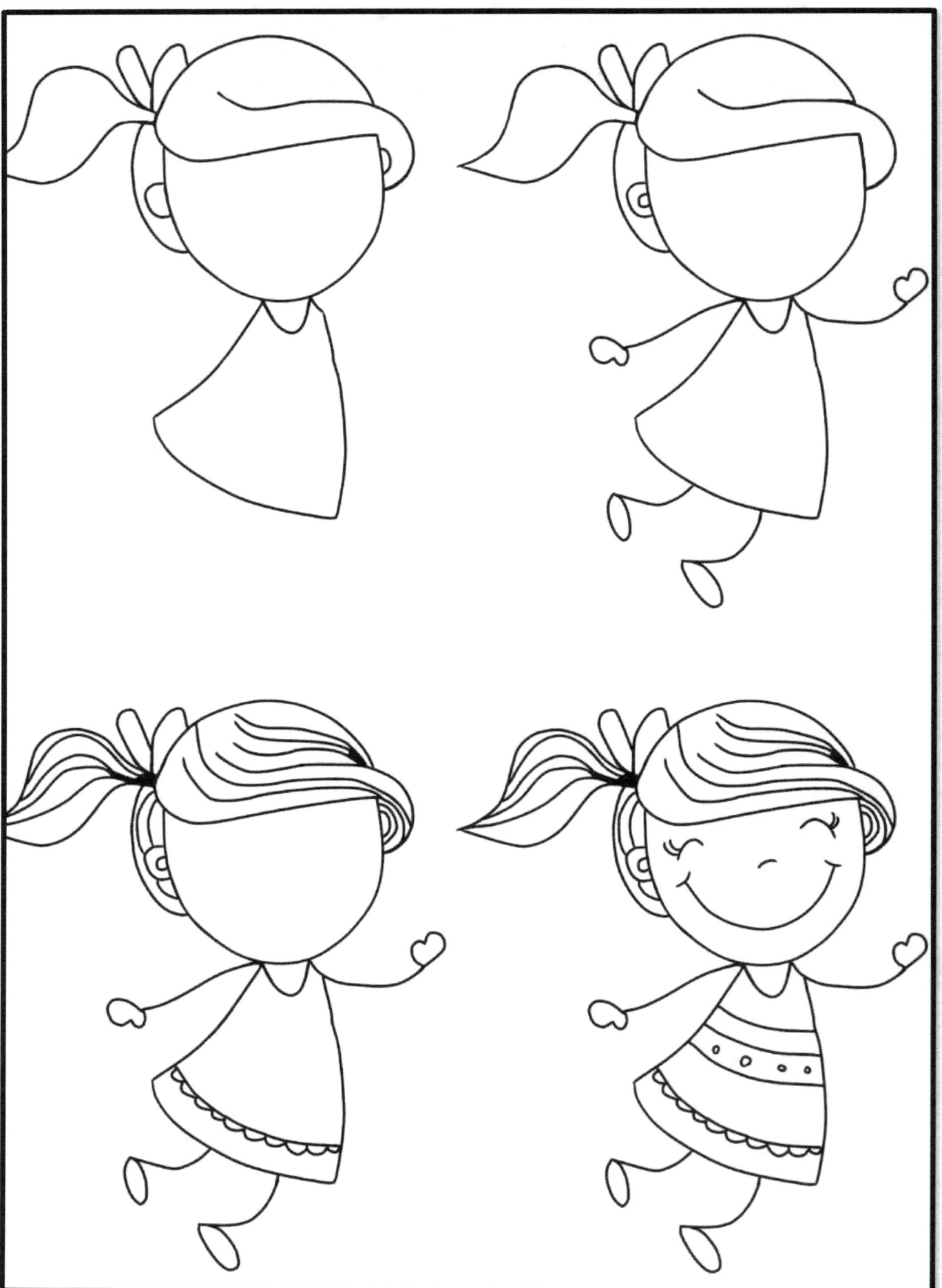

Now, it's your turn !

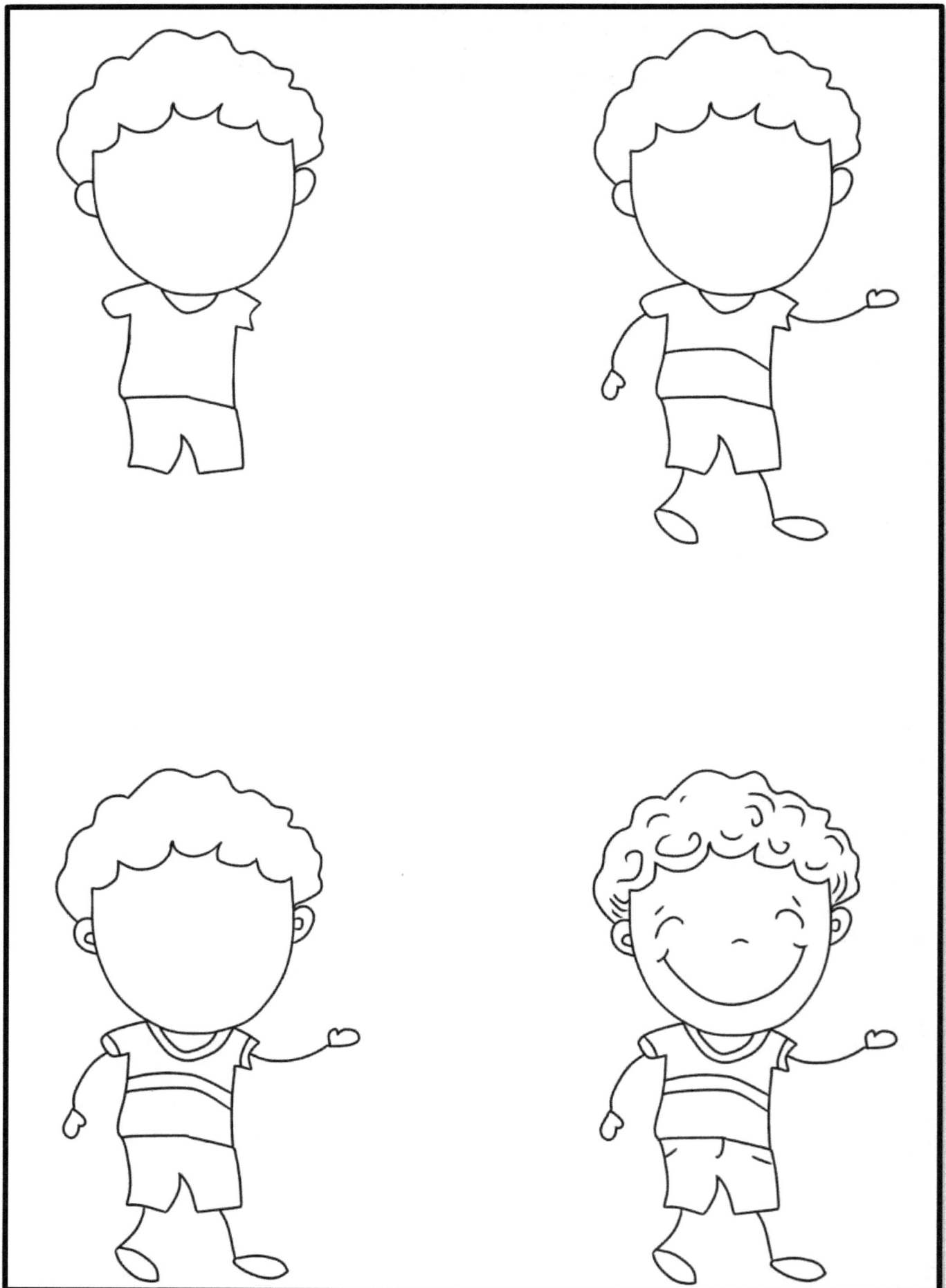

Now, it's your turn !

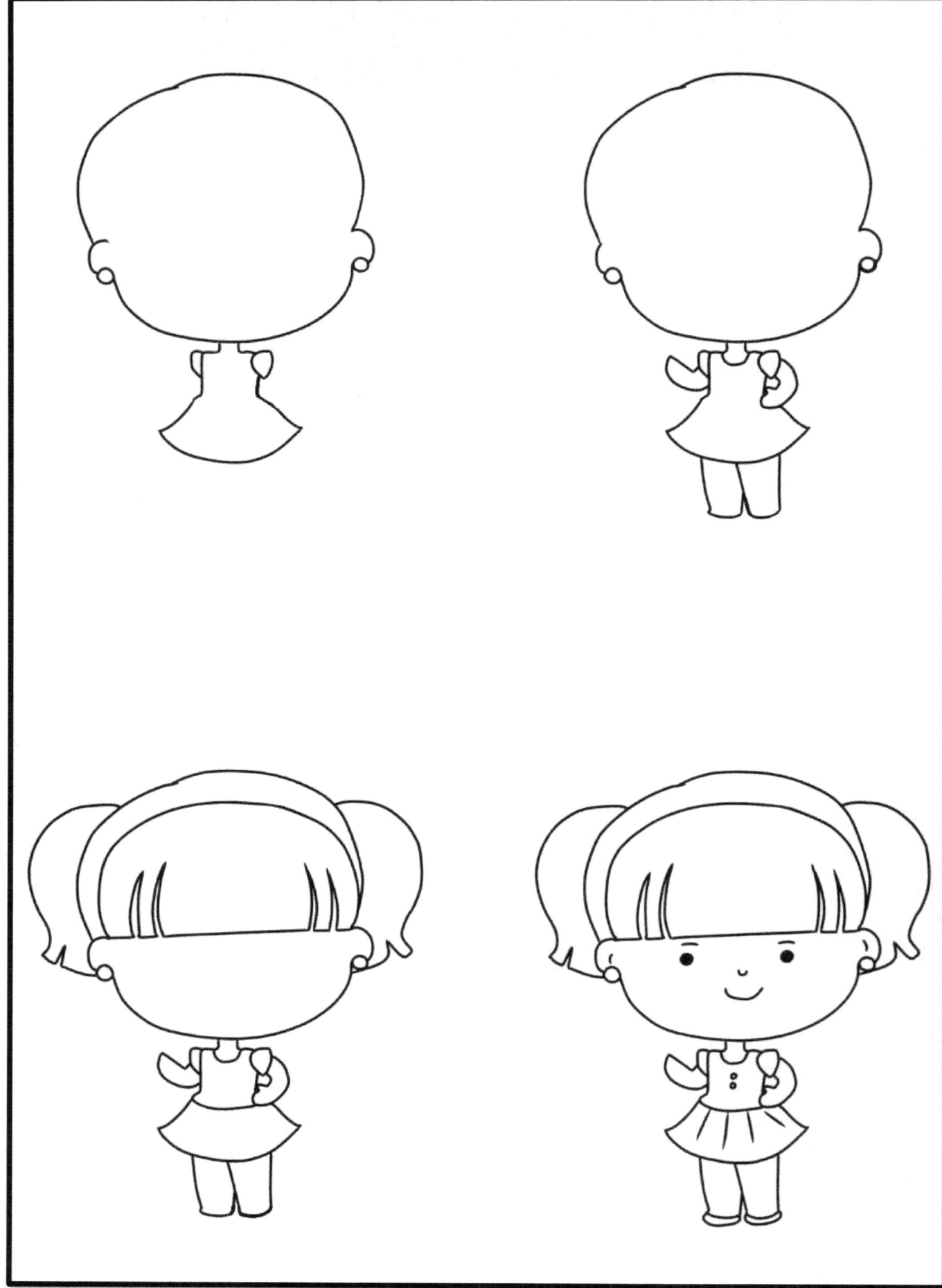

Now, it's your turn !

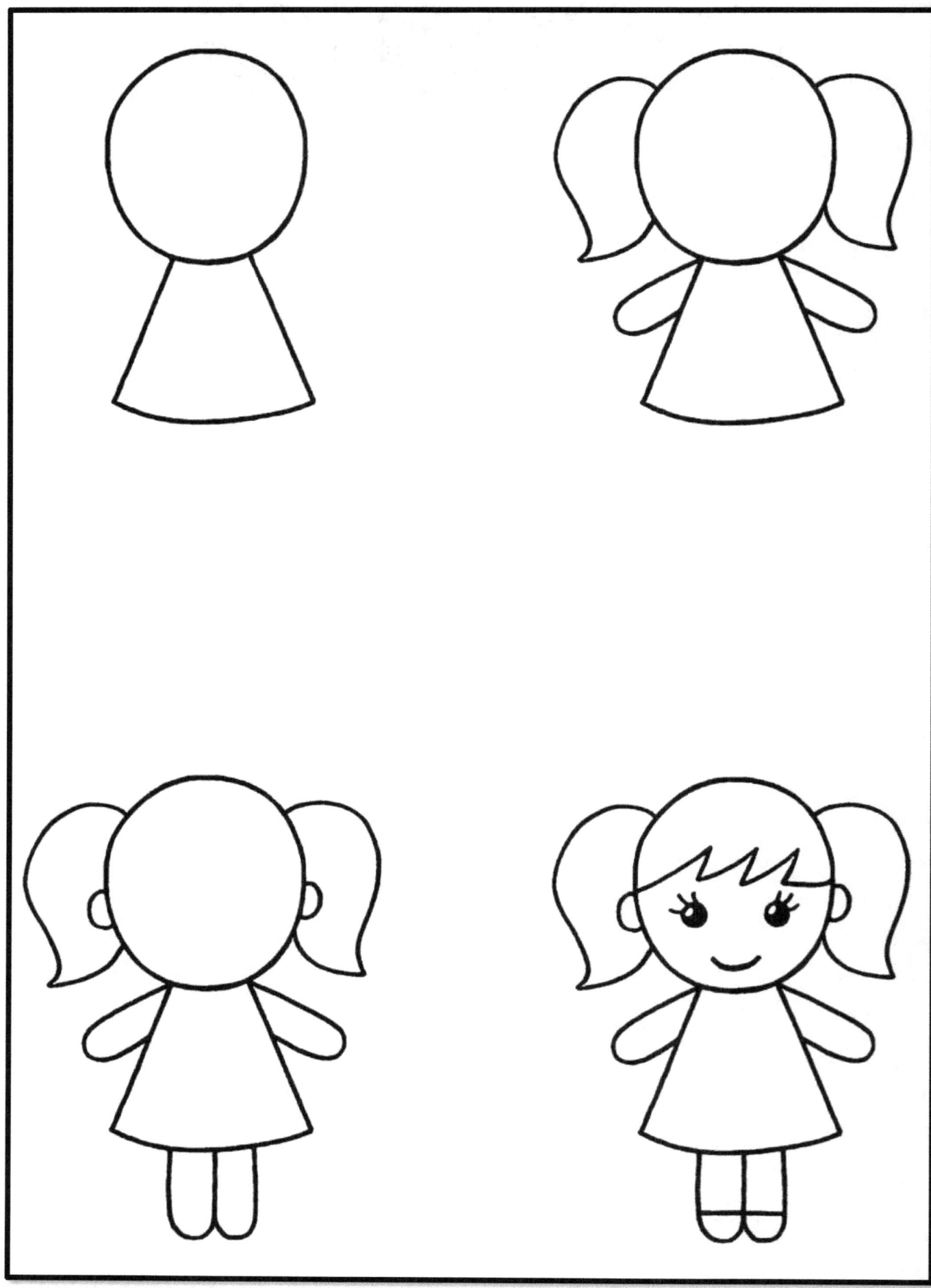

Now, it's your turn !